THE REAL READER'S QUARTERLY

Slightly Foxed

'Small World'

NO.42 SUMMER 2014

Editors Gail Pirkis and Hazel Wood
Marketing and publicity Stephanie Allen and Jennie Paterson
Subscriptions Alarys Gibson, Anna Kirk, Faith McAllister and Olivia Wilson

Cover illustration: George Devlin, *Searing Heat: Baumes de Venise*
George Devlin is a Glasgow-based artist who exhibits internationally and whose work is represented in civic, corporate and private collections worldwide, in addition to the Scottish National Gallery of Modern Art and the National Portrait Gallery of Scotland. For more about George's work please contact the Portland Gallery: edh@portlandgallery.com.

Cover fox by James Nunn

Design by Octavius Murray

Layout by Andrew Evans

Colophon and tailpiece by David Eccles

Published by Slightly Foxed Limited
53 Hoxton Square
London N1 6PB

tel 020 7033 0258
fax 0870 1991245
e-mail all@foxedquarterly.com
www.foxedquarterly.com

Slightly Foxed is published quarterly in early March, June, September and December

Printed edition: annual subscription rates (4 issues)
UK £40; Europe £48; Rest of the World £52
Printed edition & digital edition: annual subscription rates
(4 issues plus digital access to all back issues)
UK £50; Europe £58; Rest of the World £62

Single copies of this issue can be bought for £10 (UK), £12 (Europe) or £13 (Rest of the World)

All back issues are also available: for details please ring 020 7033 0258 or visit our website www.foxedquarterly.com

ISBN 978-1-906562-65-6

Printed and bound by Smith Settle, Yeadon, West Yorkshire

Contents

Contents

Simon Brett, 'Strawberries',
wood engraving from *The Fruits of Jane Austen*

From the Editors

With travel in the air, summer's a time when we think particularly of all those subscribers who read their copies of *Slightly Foxed* in far-flung places. We have subscribers in 60 countries now, and in this tenth anniversary year we'd like to say thank you once again to all of you, at home and abroad, for supporting us, and particularly to those of you who have stuck with us through – as the late publisher Antony Blond once memorably put it – thin and thin. We had an excellent anniversary party – at the Art Workers' Guild in Bloomsbury, already familiar to some of you from Readers' Day. Speeches were made, glasses were raised, and *Slightly Famous People's Foxes*, the little book we're publishing in aid of the Children's Hospital School at Great Ormond Street, was successfully launched.

The Art Workers' Guild has become a kind of home from home for *Slightly Foxed*. We like its elegant yet intimate atmosphere and the sense of a tradition that goes back to the time of William Morris. We'll be holding our annual Readers' Day there again on Friday, 7 November, and speakers this year will include the distinguished biographer (and autobiographer) Michael Holroyd; Lucy Lethbridge, whose recent book *Servants: A Downstairs View of Twentieth-century Britain* has been hugely popular; the traveller and historian Justin Marozzi, author of the recently published *Baghdad: City of Peace, City of Blood*; and Daisy Hay, whose book on the unusual courtship of Mr and Mrs Disraeli is due out next spring. It looks set to be the usual entertaining and convivial occasion, so if you'd like to join us, do get in touch. Seating is limited to 95 and tickets do go very quickly.

Since a number of you may be travelling this summer, perhaps it's the moment to remind you that digital subscriptions to *Slightly Foxed* are now available for an extra £10 a year when you renew your print subscription. As well as your four printed issues, this will give you access to the current issue and all back issues via your computer, laptop, iPad, iPhone or Android device. So enough good reading to cover any number of flights and stays in foreign parts, and no need to carry your precious print copy of *SF* with you. If you have any questions, please do phone or email Jennie.

We'd also like to draw your attention to our website. Jennie has been doing a huge amount to improve it, expand it and make it easy to use for those of you who – like us – are not perhaps entirely at ease in the digital world. On it you will now find extracts from all Slightly Foxed Editions and Slightly Foxed Cubs and all back issues of *Slightly Foxed*, and of course the invaluable index to all the contributors, books and authors we've featured. We're in the process of expanding the noticeboard section to give news of literary society talks and events, there'll be podcasts of Readers' Days and other happenings, and much more bookish information besides.

Our own latest book, Slightly Foxed Edition No. 26, is John Moore's *Portrait of Elmbury* (see p.13), the first volume in a trilogy based on the author's home of Tewkesbury – an enchanting portrait of a small English country town between the wars. Born in 1907, John Moore grew up in the town, left school at 17 and went to work for his uncle, the local auctioneer. It was an ideal vantage point for people-watching and from it, as his friend Eric Linklater observed, Moore 'received an education more liberal than that offered by most universities'. The book is a sturdy defence of the virtues of small-town life and a wonderful evocation of an England which was even then fading into the shadows. Perfect summer reading we think. We hope you'll enjoy it, wherever you are.

GAIL PIRKIS

HAZEL WOOD

Small World

MICHAEL HOLROYD

The first stories I can remember reading in my early childhood were, it seems, mainly about rabbits. But it was the illustrations rather than the words in Beatrix Potter's and Alison Uttley's books that I remember most vividly. After this there is a gap in my memory, though I suspect that Enid Blyton's prolific volumes filled much of that period. It was not until my mid-teens that I entered the exciting and adventurous worlds of Rider Haggard and Conan Doyle (not Sherlock Holmes but Brigadier Gerard was my comic hero).

Much later, after I began writing biographies, I came across several children's writers I now admire. While working on a life of the artist Augustus John, I discovered that Kathleen Hale, the creator of Orlando the Marmalade Cat, had worked as his secretary in the early 1920s. 'I felt a frisson whenever he came into the building,' she wrote. The work of dealing with unpaid bills and unanswered letters was enlivened at times by what she called 'lots of silly fun'. Out of curiosity, 'I allowed him to seduce me,' she added. 'The sex barrier down, this aberration only added a certain warmth to our friendship.' I felt something of this warmth and humour when I eventually came to read about her cat with the gooseberry eyes.

One of the significant characters in my biography of Bernard Shaw was Mrs Edith Bland. She appears on my pages as an advanced

---

Mary Norton's *The Borrowers* (1952), *The Borrowers Afield* (1955), *The Borrowers Afloat* (1959), *The Borrowers Aloft* (1961) and *The Borrowers Avenged* (1982) are available in a single paperback volume, *The Complete Borrowers* · Puffin · 720pp · £9.99 · ISBN 9780141322704.

woman who abstained from corsets, rolled her own cigarettes and called spectacularly for glasses of water at moments of drama at the Fabian Society. This 'most attractive and vivacious member of the Fabians' fell in love with Shaw and would accompany him on marathon walks across London which she hoped would end up in his lodgings and which he was determined would lead them to the British Museum. I found myself liking her so much that I began reading her books – the books for children written under her maiden name, Edith Nesbit. According to Julia Briggs's biography, her publisher was uncertain as to whether her books with their mixture of magic and social comedy were actually for children or aimed at parents who could read them aloud to their children. My belief is that they are perfect for those who, like me, are in their second childhood.

In my late seventies I have finally found for myself – that is without the aid of my biographical subjects – a children's writer whose satire on adult behaviour is subtly developed and perfectly suited to readers of all ages. This is Mary Norton, whose quintet of novels about the Borrowers was written for the most part during the 1950s. These tiny people, who mimic what they sometimes call 'Human Beans', like to think of us giants as having been put on earth to manufacture useful small objects for them. There are, for example, safety-pins (which become coat-hangers), cotton reels (on which to sit), stamps (which are placed as wonderful portraits and landscapes on their walls), toothbrushes (parts of which make excellent hair-brushes) and thimbles (from which they drink tea). All of these items and many more are borrowed or, as the giants would call it, 'stolen'.

We never see the Borrowers (or only very occasionally after drinking several glasses of Fine Madeira). But we are aware of the number of objects that vanish all the time. Something is always missing and it is this disappearance which, despite their near-invisibility, proves the existence of these Borrowers. It's elementary, my dear reader. As Sherlock Holmes explained: 'When you have eliminated the impossible, whatever remains, *however improbable*, must be the truth.'

These improbable beings have something in common with the inhabitants of the Island of Lilliput, where Gulliver was shipwrecked in the first part of Jonathan Swift's *Gulliver's Travels* (Mary Norton brings in the word 'shipwreck' to alert us to this connection). The Lilliputians were some six inches high (slightly taller, I calculate, than the Borrowers), and by recording their wars and social customs on such a diminished scale, Swift's satire made devastating ridicule of them – which is to say of us. (Another children's book, T. H. White's *Mistress Masham's Repose*, ingeniously imagines the further fate of Swift's Lilliputians.)

The three characters in Mary Norton's first book, *The Borrowers*, represent a recognizable human family. The head of the family is Pod, a most talented borrower, able when young to 'walk the length of a laid dinner-table after the gong was rung, taking a nut or sweet from every dish, and down by a fold of the table-cloth as the first people came in at the door'. His wife Homily is an ingenious cook, very house-proud – but fearful of the world outside. Their daughter Arrietty, in her early 'teens, fears nothing – not even cats. She longs to explore 'the great out-doors', to bask in the sunlight, to run through the grass, swing on twigs like the birds: in short, to be free from the gloominess of her secret life under the floors and behind the wainscots of Firbank Hall, the great Georgian house where she lives with her parents. It is a hidden, safe existence, like the lives of humans in towns and cities during the Second World War.

Daniel Macklin

In 'the golden age', when this mansion was full of wealthy people and there was much to borrow, many little people lived there: the Rain-Barrels, the Linen-Presses and the Boot-Racks, the Brown Cupboard Boys, the rather superior Harpsichords and the Hon. John Studdingtons (who lived behind a portrait of John Studdington). Pod himself belonged to the Clock family, though Homily's mother was a mere Bell-Pull – which was why she was never invited to the Overmantels' parties. These aristocratic Overmantels were a stuck-up lot who lived in the wall high up behind the mantelpiece in the morning-room where the Human Beans ate their first meal of the day. The Overmantel women were conceited tweedy creatures who admired themselves in bits of the overmantel mirror; the men were serious whisky drinkers and tobacco smokers. They lived on an eternal breakfast: 'toast and egg and snips of mushroom; sometimes sausage and crispy bacon with sips of tea and coffee'.

By the time *The Borrowers* begins, there is only one rich person and a couple of servants left in the house; and only the single Clock family of three small people. It follows that there is less to borrow, but also less chance of being seen. Nevertheless Arrietty has been seen by a 9-year-old boy and, to her parents' horror, makes friends with him. He brings the Clocks all sorts of terrific furniture from an old dolls' house in the attic; in payment for this Arrietty reads to him as he lies on his back in the garden, she standing on his shoulder, speaking into his ear and telling him when to turn the page. She improves his reading and at the same time educates herself, learning much about the mysterious world in which they all exist. But this coming together between giants and little people breaks the first rule of the Borrowers. There are good and bad people, artful and honest giants but, as Pod explains to Arrietty, they cannot be trusted: 'Steer clear of them – that's what I've always been told. No matter what they promise you. No good never really came to no one from any human being.'

And so it proves. The boy's friendship accidentally leads to the Borrowers being seen by other humans who bring in a cat, a policeman and a rat-catcher carrying his vast equipment of poisons, snares and bellows with lethal gas – in addition to some terriers and a ferret. In the chaos, Pod, Homily and Arrietty escape to the great outdoors, its beauty and its danger, where they have many adventures *Afield*, *Afloat* and *Aloft*. Wherever they go, the same rules about humans apply. Though some are friendly, others seem frightened by such tiny travesties of themselves and wish to eliminate them, while a few try to capture them in order to make money. Such is the human condition. There is a reference in these adventures to Henry Fielding's mock-heroic farce *Tom Thumb*, who was sadly eaten by a cow, a *Tragedy of Tragedies* that brought tears of rare laughter to Jonathan Swift.

What reignites the ingenuity and humour of these volumes is the creation of a supreme Borrower of Borrowers, the amazing Spiller. He doesn't know how old he is and has no memory of his family beyond his mother telling him at breakfast: 'A dreadful spiller, that's what you are, aren't you?' So Dreadful Spiller he remains: an outdoors borrower who, with his earth-dark face and bright black eyes, is a master of concealment, melting into the background, disappearing fast and becoming invisible. He is a miraculous hunter. He owns a couple of boats – an old wooden knife-box which he cleverly guides along the river for long journeys carrying strange borrowed cargoes, and the bottom half of an aluminium soap-case, slightly dented, for more modest expeditions. He is fearless, but suddenly shy when saving the lives of the Clock family. His teasing smile greatly attracts Arrietty, for whom he embodies the whole wide out-of-doors world.

Spiller leads the Clocks to Homily's brother's family, which enables Mary Norton to balance self-reliance against family life (so many people, so many rules, so much for show and so little for use). 'Poor Spiller,' thinks Arrietty. 'Solitary they called him . . . Perhaps that's what's the matter with me.' Mary Norton is not sentimental about families. She seems to prefer the individual enterprise of Spiller and Arrietty who are both loners.

Four of Mary Norton's Borrowers' books were published within nine years. Then, after an interval of twenty-one years (and ten years before her death), she brought out her final volume, *The Borrowers Avenged*, in 1982. It begins where *The Borrowers Aloft* ended – as if no time has passed. Having made a complicated escape from an attic prison by balloon (an achievement overlooked by Richard Holmes in his book of balloons, *Falling Upwards*), the Clocks are led by Spiller on an adventurous journey to an ancient, overgrown rectory. Here, amid danger, excitement and surprise, they encounter new and old friends and enemies. One question remains: what will be the future for Arrietty? Will it be with Spiller, the borrower who belongs to the outdoors, or Peagreen, an attractive young borrower with a charming smile, who was abandoned by the Overmantels and belongs to the indoor life? Perhaps this could be decided through a new literary prize written in competition by admiring borrowers of Mary Norton's characters.

MICHAEL HOLROYD has written the Lives of Bernard Shaw, Augustus John, Lytton Strachey and himself. He is half Swedish and partly Irish – which may account for some of his literary judgements (Mary Norton spent her last years in Ireland).

Down Tewkesbury Way

JEREMY LEWIS

'I have written a book which gives me much pleasure. It is a kind of full-length portrait of a small country town – this small town – between the wars. The sort of life that will never come back,' John. Moore told T. H. White in the summer of 1945. Already a well-established and prolific professional writer, Moore had written *Portrait of Elmbury* in six weeks after leaving the Admiralty Press Division in London to return to his home town of Tewkesbury, and it was to form the first part of a trilogy based on Tewkesbury and its surrounding villages. *Portrait of Elmbury* (1945) and *Brensham Village* (1946) were both published by Collins and *The Blue Field* followed in 1948: the names of places and people had been changed, but the disguise was lightly worn.

Portrait of Elmbury got the trilogy off to a flying start: I read it in hospital, waiting to be operated on, and it did me no end of good; so much so that I persuaded my wife to get hold of its successors so I could remain in this magical, vanished world. It's a book of Dickensian energy and flamboyance, sturdy in its defence of small-town life against metropolitan condescension, and peopled by vibrant eccentrics, including a waterlogged, heavy-drinking Colonel who spends his days shooting ducks while semi-submerged in reed beds before propping up the bar at the Shakespeare, one of the twenty-eight pubs serving a population of 5,000; Pistol, Bardolph and Nym, the town's drunken reprobates, tottering along at the back of any procession and lowering the tone as they go; and their improbable friend the Town Crier, 'a very frail-looking old man with a white beard and a thin quavery voice'.

Born in 1907, John Moore grew up in Tewkesbury, and was to spend most of his life in and around the little market town on the Severn, best known for what Pevsner described as 'probably the largest and finest Romanesque tower in England'. Moore's family was 'bourgeois and ordinary': doctors, lawyers and auctioneers who 'had lived in and about Elmbury for so long that they seemed to have proprietary rights in the place', and he himself 'belonged to the place as a limb belongs to the body'. As a child, Moore lived in Tudor House, 'the loveliest house in Elmbury', which 'looked across a wide main street upon the filthiest slum I have ever set eyes on in England', consisting of a series of 'tottering hunchback cottages', each more squalid than the last. 'The ragged women, the drunken men, the screaming wanton wretches, the rickety children, were more real to us than many of our relations,' Moore tells us, and the drunken Black Sal and her fellow slum-dwellers were to loom large in his pages.

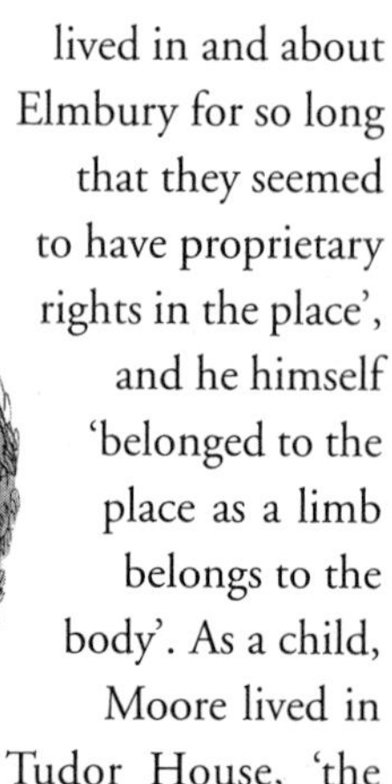

Daniel Macklin

Elmbury was never a beauty spot, Moore insists, and he came to resent the fact that, in the late Thirties, it became a magnet for charabancs from the Midlands, and the Hogarthian Double Alley was tidied up to keep the tourists happy: 'beauty and ugliness grew up side by side and merged into a single entity, indivisible and unique, in which you could no more easily separate and distinguish those two qualities than you could winnow out the good and evil in the heart of man'. He relished its extraordinary diversity:

> the rich seething hotchpotch of a thousand ingredients . . . Elmbury was a small town, and such are generally supposed to be dull, and to be associated with aspidistras, and to infect the souls of their inhabitants with something mean and crabbed and petty, with ignorant 'provincialism' and with something specially reprehensible and circumscribed called a 'small-town mentality'. But Elmbury wasn't like that at all. It had infinite variety. It was splendid and it was sordid; but it certainly wasn't dull.

Moore was sent to a nearby prep school, where he fell under the benign influence of Mr Chorlton, a bachelor schoolmaster of the best kind, an expert on Greek verse and Lepidoptera who had played cricket for Oxford and Somerset, and who resurfaces in the later volumes. From there he went on to Malvern: like C. S. Lewis and Raymond Mortimer, he claimed to have loathed his time at this 'hateful' institution, but it seems that the then headmaster encouraged him to write, while a colleague spotted his burgeoning interest in natural history. (I remember him coming to talk to the school in the late Fifties, so he can't have disliked it that much.)

He left school at 17, and went to work for his uncle as an auctioneer in Tewkesbury. As his friend Eric Linklater later wrote – and as *Portrait of Elmbury* makes plain – 'from the clients of a country auctioneer he received an education more liberal than that offered by most universities'. Nor did he neglect his own education: Mr Chorlton had imbued him with a love of Greek literature; he read poetry by the yard; he knew about butterflies and wild flowers, and he could shoot, ride and sail; he even learned to fly, which enabled him to join the Fleet Air Arm at the outbreak of war. Good-looking and convivial, 'I was a tough young rascal with my head full of poetry and the rest of my interest divided pretty equally between horses, fishes, motor-bikes and girls.'

But he wanted, above all, to be a writer. He made his way into print at the age of 16 and wrote whenever he could, in between flogging off the chattels of bankrupt farmers or estimating the value of a herd of cattle or a warehouse full of old furniture, perched in one corner of his uncle's dusty old office, surrounded by the leather-bound records of sales going back to the eighteenth century. He amassed his fair share of rejection letters, but his second novel found a publisher. 'Write! That's a hobby, my boy, not a profession!' his auctioneer uncle remonstrated when he handed in his notice to embark on the life of a freelance writer.

He went to Spain during the Civil War, working as a journalist; he spent some time in London, but found both the city and its literary circles uncongenial. London literary folk were amazed that he preferred to 'bury' himself in 'a dead-alive country town'; Moore, for his part, thought the inhabitants of Bloomsbury 'as conventional as the heroes and heroines of their novels', wraith-like figures compared with 'the full-blooded exuberant company at the Shakespeare or the Swan'. On his return to Tewkesbury after some years away, he wrote:

> Emotion seemed larger here, pleasures were keener, sorrows sharper, men's laughter was more boisterous, jokes were funnier, the tragedy was more profound and the comedy more riotous, the huge fantasy of life was altogether more fantastic. London, for all its street lights, was a twilit world; Elmbury, on a murky February evening, seemed as bright as a stage.

Moore kept writing through it all, turning his hand to fiction, poetry, scripts and – during his time with the Admiralty Press Division – wartime propaganda (his colleagues included Ludovic Kennedy and Nicholas Monsarrat). John Buchan was an early and faithful admirer, as was Compton Mackenzie, later to become a close friend; he made a good living, but, in Eric Linklater's temperate words, 'Moore was never a fashionable writer, nor made any attempt to catch those errant breezes which may carry cleverer men into a climate warmed by intellectual approval and popular applause. On his own themes, however, and within his own territory, he was a very good writer, and his territory was England – an England which has vanished, or is vanishing, but deserves a loving remembrance . . .'

Richard Church – another neglected writer, and for a time Moore's editor at J. M. Dent – once wrote of his friend that 'not since Richard Jefferies died have we had a spokesman of the English country life, the very spirit of place, who can conjure the smells, sights and sounds as well as the mysteries, silences and portents of night and day down on the farm, along the winding lanes, and through the lush woodland as John Moore does', while Harold Nicolson acclaimed him as 'one of our best writers on the English countryside'.

All this is true enough, but what one treasures most in *Portrait of Elmbury* are its inhabitants: the duck-shooting, whisky-toting Colonel, with his pulsating red nose, his 'badger-grizzled walrus moustache and little twinkling blue eyes'; Miss Benedict, the censorious barmaid of the Shakespeare, who disapproved of her customers' drunken ways and knew all the secrets of the town, and without whom the pub would never be the same again; Mr Rendcome, the implacable and incorruptible editor of the *Elmbury Intelligencer*, tireless in his exposure of municipal misdeeds, and forever harking back to a vanished golden age; the dashing young farmers, riding helter-skelter across country in pursuit of a bet or a girl; the town's small army of odd-job men, who could turn their hand to whatever needed to be done, from plum-picking and cutting osiers to salmon-netting and rick-cutting, and who 'acted as a leaven on the whole community'; the young men of Elmbury marching off to war in 1914, many of them never to return.

John Moore died in July 1967, leaving his widow, Lucile, to sort out his debts and liabilities. As well as being a popular and successful writer, he had been one of the founders of the Cheltenham Literary Festival, an effective Chairman of the Society of Authors, and a determined defender of old Tewkesbury, but he has yet to make it into the *Dictionary of National Biography.* He deserves to be far better remembered: a lyrical yet level-headed combination of autobiography and topography, *Portrait of Elmbury* is his finest achievement, and the book with which to revive his reputation.

JEREMY LEWIS's most recent book, *Shades of Greene: One Generation of an English Family*, is now available in paperback. He is researching a biography of David Astor, the former editor of the *Observer*, to be published by Jonathan Cape.

Sophia Fairclough and Me

SOPHIE BREESE

I was first introduced to Sophia Fairclough in 1985 by my new English teacher, the kind who came to lessons without notes and charmed those susceptible to such charm with his raw excitement for good writing. Sophia herself, although fictional, was immediately real to me: a quirky, self-deprecating, parentless artist who took people at face value and made many mistakes as a result. I loved her. I loved her naïvety, her optimism, even her self-destructive behaviour. I wanted to shake her into action but I also wanted to *be* her. She became an unlikely heroine for me, for though I planned to be a writer when I was older rather than an artist, I was quite prepared to suffer, to be poor, to live off tinned soup, even to fail in love, if these experiences enriched my writing.

I remember my first meeting with Sophia well. As usual we fell silent as Mr Fitzmaurice came into the room. He was still on trial, though I had long since made up my mind about him. He was a small man with big hair; he always wore black but not polo necks, so I don't think he was an existentialist, despite the constant smell of cigarettes. But he was a teacher who loved his subject and that was all that mattered to me. And then he began to tell us about one of his favourite writers, Barbara Comyns, reading us the first page of Sophia's story, *Our Spoons Came from Woolworths* (1950), as a taster.

I was hooked: she was my near namesake, the title of the novel was

---

Barbara Comyns, *Our Spoons Came from Woolworths* (1950) · Virago · Pb · 208pp · £8.99 · ISBN 9781844089277; *The Vet's Daughter* (1959) · Virago · Pb · 176pp · £8.99 · ISBN 9781844088386. *A Touch of Mistletoe* (1967) is out of print.

unforgettable, and the writing was completely different from anything I had read before. After the lesson I went straight to the library and found the novel in its green Virago casing with a grotesque Stanley Spencer woman's bottom looming out of the front cover. I read it that weekend, cried a lot when it was finished, and over the next few months bought or borrowed all the books by Barbara Comyns that were in print.

Our Spoons Came from Woolworths is the semi-autobiographical second novel of a rather glamorous-looking woman with painted eyebrows and rosebud lips; a black-and-white film star rather than an impoverished writer. From a once rich, then poor family, married first to an artist and later – apparently – to a spy, Comyns travelled, washed plates, bred poodles, painted, wrote and came to the attention of Graham Greene. There is not a great deal else to be found about her, apart from a typically witty five-page autobiographical introduction to the 1980 reprint of a later novel, *The Vet's Daughter*, and few people seem to have heard of her. Yet those who do know her writing have, like me, read everything by her in a rather obsessive fashion.

There are two things that are remarkable about *Spoons*. The first is the story itself, with its unselfconscious fairy-tale theme. Sophia is a kind of Cinderella, having lived in bedsits since she was 17 for reasons not explained. We discover, towards the end, that her father died after swallowing a wasp but we learn little else about her pre-novel life. The story charts her journey towards a state of being 'not unhappy', as she tells us on the first page, but this is typical Sophia understatement: at the end of the novel a prince of sorts does come.

Along the way we witness the collapse of her marriage to a deeply selfish and quite probably talentless artist, the birth of her first child, an affair with a man with a ridiculous name, and a variety of sometimes funny, often tragic events. What is odd is that the ending does not come as a cliché, perhaps because there is nothing overly thought-through about the novel, no sense that Comyns has planned each section carefully and deliberately alluded to other literary texts. Jane Eyre gets several mentions but this is not a reworking of Brontë's story: Jane is simply a character to whom Sophia relates. One might describe Comyns's approach as artless and there is something very refreshing in this, particularly when so much contemporary fiction seems so clever for the sake of being clever.

Comyns's writing style in both *Spoons* and her other novels is also unusual. I have often tried to describe her books to friends and have always found it difficult. On the face of it, there is a simplicity about her writing, a straightforwardness which is almost child-like. This is partly because Comyns is telling the story through Sophia who is herself naïve, particularly about love and the facts of life, exposing, rather poignantly, her motherless state. Each pregnancy comes as a surprise, even a shock; and deaths are often described in asides. But this childlike world-view means that Sophia's narration is without pretension and allows her to record incidents without the judgement that a more sophisticated narrator would bring.

The effect is both humorous and unsettling. Sophia seriously considers leaving her baby and pram attached to the railings outside her office so she can return to work once the baby is born – an indication of her inability to understand how the world works. More uncomfortable, though, is her graphic description of a painful and lonely labour. Sophia is treated badly, is given no information, and is not allowed to see her new baby for some time. She appears to feel no bitterness towards her husband who never wanted a child, but blames herself for giving birth at all. This sequence of events is made all the more disturbing by an author's note on the copyright page to the effect that Chapters 10, 11 and 12 (the birth) are 'true'.

This sense of dislocation from her life, both as a narrator and as a participant, creates a style that borders on the surreal, which is the best word I can find to describe Comyns's writing. Vicky, the heroine of a later novel, *A Touch of Mistletoe* (1967), is given a ticket to the Surrealist Exhibition at the Burlington Galleries, a real event in 1936 which featured the work of such artists as Dalí and Miró. Vicky writes that she 'visited it over and over again and it was as if [she] had been given an extra eye to see with and ordinary objects took on new shapes'.

This surrealism goes further than just the writing style. Comyns creates a world in which magical events are given the same credence as real ones; to me she seems an early magical realist, prefiguring the work of writers such as Angela Carter. Just as Sophia fails to comment on her husband's infidelity or her constant and acute poverty, she does not express any surprise when she sees her mother's ghost. Despite being in acute pain, the pregnant Sophia decides not to wake her husband until her dead mother, on the rocking-chair in front of the bed, tells her it is time to go to hospital. The reader is expected to accept the truth of her mother's presence because when he awakes her husband acknowledges it too. For me, this is a particularly sad passage because it takes a voice from the grave to insist that Sophia assume responsibility for herself.

The unworldly is given a much more dramatic rôle in *The Vet's Daughter* (1959). Re-reading all Comyns's novels together for the first time in about fifteen years, I must conclude – reluctantly and with apologies for my disloyalty to *Spoons* – that it is also probably her best, rightly listed in the *Observer*'s 'Ten Best Neglected Literary Classics' in 2011. Much more controlled, much barer in style, the novel is a shocking account of the economic and social powerlessness of women in the period before the Second World War. All her novels deal with this theme but in *The Vet's Daughter*, Alice Rowlands's life is so grotesque and emotionally deprived that her only escape is literally to levitate out of her circumstances.

It is also one of the most moving accounts of loss and grief that I have read: my own mother died a couple of years ago, and so for me the description of the death of Alice's mother was very powerful. Alice is angry, confused, rejected, distraught, wanting it to be over soon because it is so painful for all concerned yet desperate for this period never to end. Mrs Rowlands tells Alice stories about herself, particularly about her childhood, as she lies in bed waiting to die, some sad, some happy; my mother did the same with me. It was one of the hardest times of my life but the shared knowledge of my mother's imminent departure brought the two of us closer than we had ever been before. In *The Vet's Daughter*, Comyns captures that deathbed intensity between mother and daughter perfectly.

And yet, and yet, I come back to *Our Spoons Came from Woolworths*. I have read it at least ten times; it is my comfort read of choice despite some discomfort along the way; a novel of aspiration and inspiration. It is a reminder of the end of my innocent love of English; the moment when I began to recognize the difference between the superb stories of page-turning novelists such as Monica Dickens and Lynne Reid Banks and the superb and unusual story-*telling* of literary writers like Elizabeth Taylor and Rosamond Lehmann.

It is also a reminder of the importance of this English teacher to me and of several others who introduced to me similarly life-changing texts: Miss Shadlock who gave the 11-year-old me *Jane Eyre*; Mrs Babuta who showed me, aged 17, the rose garden in 'Burnt Norton'. It was because of such teachers that I became an English teacher myself: I wanted to enthuse about my favourite novels and encourage others to fall in love with words; I wanted to teach like these teachers; and, perhaps rather egotistically, I wanted to inspire young readers and writers. Curiously I never quite felt able to teach *Spoons*; I taught Lehmann's *Invitation to the Waltz* and Antonia White's *Frost in May*, but I kept Barbara Comyns to myself, sneaking her in only on booklists for my students' general reading. Until now.

SOPHIE BREESE has been involved with words since her first encounter with Sophia Fairclough, teaching English literature for some years. She now lives in the Périgord, where she is writing a novel, teaching online and learning how to garden.

Living Art

MARK HAWORTH-BOOTH

One of the most charming and illuminating memoirs I know is also the largest. *A Way of Life: Kettle's Yard* by Jim Ede, published by Cambridge University Press in 1984, is almost a foot square and over an inch thick. It is large because its author was above all a visual man, and he wanted to give due prominence to the many subtly toned black-and-white photographs among which his words gracefully flow. The book is like an ideal visit to Kettle's Yard, the unique house filled with art and objects Ede created in Cambridge. Through Kettle's Yard and the way of life it embodies, Ede (1895–1990) influenced generations of Cambridge undergraduates and many artists.

I was one of those undergraduates. I had gone up to Cambridge to read English in 1963. I remember choosing a reproduction of Rembrandt's *The Mill* from the college loan collection to give my set of rooms a touch of gloomy distinction. It must have been in my second term that a friend told me about a man who opened his house to visitors several afternoons a week to view his collection – he even allowed undergraduates to borrow pictures. My callow imagination conjured up a flashy aesthete in a tall town house, probably with an agenda extending beyond the love of art.

Still I was intrigued, and soon my friend and I were standing outside the modest honey-coloured cottages off Castle Street (near Magdalene College) that Jim had transformed into a home for himself and his wife Helen and a place for art. The bell-pull was a ring of

---

Jim Ede, *A Way of Life: Kettle's Yard* (1984)
Kettle's Yard · Hb · 256pp · £49.95 · ISBN 9780907074571

cork, the first indication of Jim's talent for beachcombing. A chime within brought the owner to the door – a slim, white-haired man with bright blue eyes, wearing a denim-blue jacket. We heard ourselves being welcomed in a musical voice. Jim always wrote down the names of his visitors on a small piece of card kept in his top pocket as an *aide-mémoire*, careful to spell them accurately and learn them before his guests left. Another friend recalls Jim enunciating the name of a blond-haired visitor – 'David Hockney, is that with an e or without?'

Jim would usually wait until he had a little group assembled to show round. As we stood there, Kettle's Yard began to reveal its themes: light-filled domestic spaces, white walls, plain wooden surfaces, some decorated with circles of pebbles, fabrics in cream or oatmeal, hand-painted china in corner cupboards, fine old glass gleaming on shelves and harmoniously arranged masterpieces of modern painting and sculpture. I doubt that I'd got much beyond the Impressionists at that time. Now I was introduced to the paintings of Christopher Wood, Ben Nicholson, Winifred Nicholson, Alfred Wallis, David Jones and Joan Miró, to the abstract collages of Italo Valenti, the optical art of Vardanega and sculptures by Henri Gaudier-Brzeska, Brancusi and Henry Moore.

Some of the works were charged with great power, such as Gaudier's bronze *Bird swallowing a fish* (1914) which Jim linked to the mechanized killing of the First World War (in which the young sculptor died). I also relished the little game Jim played by placing a lemon on a pewter charger below an almost abstract still life with fruit by Ben Nicholson. The actual still life and the painted one interacted, showing how the beauty of real things could be matched and intensified: the patches of coloured paint were simultaneously pure pigment and absolute apple.

I left Kettle's Yard that afternoon knowing I'd discovered something much better than a private house or a public gallery. I'd found a place in which art and life achieved a rich harmony and balance. I

QVIA·PER·IN
CARNATI·
VERBI·MYS
TERIVM·N
OVA·MEN
TIS·NOST
RÆ·OCVLIS·
LVX·TVÆ·

also came away with a framed pen-and-ink drawing to hang in my rooms. It was a Gaudier of an *Amazone* riding a spirited steed. 'Don't hang it in sunlight. Just bring it back at the end of term,' Jim said as he entered my name and college in his book of loans.

Before long I became a habitué. I realized that if you hung around at the end of visiting time, you might be asked to stay to tea. Then you would meet the lovely Helen, with her white fringe and Scottish brogue. She and Jim had met in Edinburgh soon after the First World War and married in 1921. I learned how delicious marmalade is if produced cold from the fridge and served at teatime. I also gathered that Jim was a regular hospital visitor who would sit and talk to patients who had no friends or family visiting them. And each evening at 6 p.m. Jim would ring the bell at St Peter's, the tiny church nearby, to sound the Angelus. The Edes' lives were full of practical piety, woven into the aesthetics of living. This is beautifully captured in the text and many photographs in *A Way of Life*, but especially in this passage:

> Winifred Nicholson taught me much about the fusing of art and daily living, and Ben Nicholson that traffic in Piccadilly had the rhythm of a ballet and a game of tennis the perfection of an old master. Life with them at once seemed lively, satisfying and special.

I began to learn about Jim. He had attended the Newlyn Arts School and then the Slade before going to the Tate as assistant to its director in 1921. While he readily befriended the adventurous young painters of his generation, the Tate remained aloof. Eventually, in 1936, Jim and Helen moved to Tangiers – from where he went on lecture tours to the US – and later to the Loire valley. They settled in Cambridge and began making Kettle's Yard out of four condemned cottages in 1956. By my time as an undergraduate, it was well established. I was startled to find that Jim had been offering Kettle's Yard as a gift to the University of Cambridge for several years, but was always turned down because of worries over expense and questions about whether enough people would visit a place that seemed very modest compared to the mighty Fitzwilliam Museum.

In 1966, a fellow undergraduate, James Fraser, and I devised a petition urging the university to accept the gift. Jim pointed us towards known fans of Kettle's Yard, including distinguished scientists, as well as enthusiastic fellows, undergraduates and other well-wishers. He mentioned E. M. Forster and I arranged to visit the great novelist. His rooms at King's were on the first floor of A staircase, on the left as you enter the college from King's Parade. Like many other undergraduates, I had read his *The Longest Journey* (1907) – partly set in Cambridge – with acute interest, identifying completely with its troubled protagonist Rickie.

Forster waved me to a chaise-longue, on one end of which were that morning's opened letters, their envelopes crumpled on the carpet. He offered me water biscuits and said yes of course he knew Jim – Jim had been on the fringes of Bloomsbury in the Twenties – and of course he would sign. He did so in the way the elderly do, placing the nib of his pen on the paper with deliberation and then making the characters in a desperate rush. I was elated. A week or so later I received a postcard from Aldeburgh. It had been written on Forster's behalf by someone with a firmer hand. The message ran: 'I now realize what your petition is about. I am so glad I signed it.'

Another signature was that of an undergraduate Jim said I should be sure to contact. I left a sheet for Nicholas Serota and soon received it back duly signed. A selection of signatories' names was published in the *Cambridge Review* and an article appeared in the student paper *Varsity*. I went down that June but stayed in touch with Jim. On 28 October 1966 he wrote: 'I'm glad at last to be able to announce what I expect you have already heard, that the University has accepted Kettle's Yard and all that is in it, stones and all (I've kept a bed or two) . . .'

The University went on to buy a piece of adjoining land and, with

Jim's participation, commissioned Sir Leslie Martin to build an elegant gallery extension. It was opened in May 1970 by the Prince of Wales, then an undergraduate at Trinity. An inaugural concert was given by Jacqueline du Pré and Daniel Barenboim. Under a series of inspired directors, Kettle's Yard has been further extended with a separate exhibition gallery but always in the spirit of the four cottages transformed by Jim, which remain the aesthetic core.

Helen and Jim left Cambridge for Edinburgh in 1973 and Helen died there in 1977. I visited Jim in his new quarters in Morningside. I remember calling on him when I was due to give a public lecture at the University of Edinburgh and nervously saying, as I left him at his front gate, 'I hope they like me.' 'I'm sure they'll love you,' he replied. When he became frail, Jim moved into a ground-floor flat in the house of one of his daughters. I visited him there and found that he'd contrived to make his rooms into a mini Kettle's Yard, using space, light, natural materials, well-chosen art works and some good pebbles.

Some of us went on from Cambridge to work in museums and galleries. I feel sure that Sir Nicholas Serota, CH, as he now is, would agree that although we may have enlarged the numbers involved in looking at art of many different kinds, no public galleries match the quality of the experience offered by Kettle's Yard. There we find not only objects but a whole way of life.

I found myself thinking of Jim only a few days ago as I contemplated the rather grubby slabs of stone set in the lawn between our front door and the garden gate. A passage in Jim's memoir describes how he scoured similar slabs at his house in Hampstead in the Thirties and brought them to a shine. I could never emulate Jim's strenuously aesthetic way of life but I'm so pleased I got to know him and it.

MARK HAWORTH-BOOTH worked at the Victoria and Albert Museum from 1970 to 2004, where he served as senior curator of photographs. He now lives in North Devon near some excellent pebble beaches.

Where the Blue Really Begins

SUE GEE

In the summer of 1965, I hitchhiked with two school friends to Greece. We had just done our A levels, with mixed results. In Corfu, we all met our first boyfriends: likewise. What cast the real spell, over all of us nice Surrey girls, were the Greek islands. And the two books we read in those enchanted weeks offered the most intense marriage of literature and experience that I can remember.

After our hot, arduous journey through France and Italy, by car and (mostly) lorry, we had made the night crossing from Brindisi, in south-east Italy, to a Corfu first seen in a silvery dawn. Almost thirty years earlier, in the spring of 1937, Lawrence Durrell had made a similar crossing with his wife, a painter. They were young, and free-spirited; in Kalami, in the north of the island, they took an old fisherman's whitewashed house overlooking the sea. She began to paint. He began a journal.

> Somewhere between Calabria and Corfu the blue really begins . . . Once you strike out from the flat and desolate Calabrian mainland towards the sea, you are aware of a change in the heart of things . . . of islands coming out of the darkness to meet you . . . aware not so much of a landscape coming to meet you invisibly over those blue miles of water as of a climate . . . Other countries

---

Lawrence Durrell, *Prospero's Cell* (1945 · 192pp · ISBN 9780571201655) and *Bitter Lemons of Cyprus* (1957 · 288pp · ISBN 9780571201556) are both published in paperback by Faber at £7.99.

> may offer you discoveries in manners or lore or landscape; Greece offers you something harder – the discovery of yourself.

Prospero's Cell (1945) is the first of three books charting Durrell's long love affair with Greek islands. Begun in notebook entries, it was, he explains in the Preface, finally composed in Alexandria – the setting for *The Alexandria Quartet*, novels which in retrospect seem to have cast their own spell over my whole generation. There he had fled, as the war took hold of Greece. 'In those dark winters of 1941–2 Corcyra [as he always refers to it, anglicizing the Greek Kerkyra] seemed a place I would never see again in this life.' The book was a huge success. 'And its continuing success down the years has always touched me like a sort of confirmation that my dreams of being a writer when I was young were worth holding on to.'

In our floppy straw hats and wraparound cheesecloth skirts, the three of us sat on the steps of the youth hostel outside Corfu town, our sandalled feet in the dust, and drank in Durrell's miraculous prose.

> You wake one morning in late autumn and notice that everything has changed: the sky shines more deeply pearl, and the sun rises like a ball of blood – for the peaks of the Albanian hills are touched with snow. The sea has become leaden and sluggish, and the olives a deep platinum grey. Fires smoke in the villages, and the breath of Maria as she passes with her sheep to the headland, is faintly white upon the air . . . sheep bells clonk dully around her.

Like Durrell, we were in a timeless landscape of cypress, olive groves and sun-warmed stone, of donkeys laden with firewood and old men sitting outside cafés on wooden chairs. Like him, we walked through mountain villages and along the coast, and saw the shadowy outlines of the mountains of Albania across the sea. And, as he had done, we visited the church of St Spiridon where, in a much-kissed silver casket, lie the remains of the island's patron saint, still performing miracles today. 'St Spiridon', wrote Durrell, 'is still awake after nearly two thousand years.'

Other spirits preside over Corfu, as they preside over the whole of our understanding of Ancient Greece: Euclid, Socrates, Plato, evoked here mostly through imagery: 'And now the stars are shining down frost-blown and taut upon this pure Euclidean surface.' 'The divine Plato', a friend tells Durrell, 'once said that in Greece you see god with his compasses and dividers.'

But Homer and the *Odyssey* are also layered into the landscape, and Durrell makes pilgrimages to the three towns which contend for the meeting place of Ulysses and Nausicaa. 'Last and most likely is Paleocastrizza, drenched in the silver of olives on the north-western coast. The little bay lies in a trance, drugged with its own extraordinary perfection.'

Then there is Shakespeare, and *The Tempest*, about which Durrell's new scholarly Greek friends have complicated theories. Was Shakespeare thinking of Corfu when he wrote his last great play? And, finally, there is Edward Lear, who stayed here in the 1850s and early 1860s, who played the piano, painted and exhibited gloomy watercolours, and wrote beguiling letters home. 'My life here has gone on very sklombionbiously on the whole . . .'

All this, with Durrell's rhapsodic response to place and people, is richly interwoven with political history. Corfu was colonized many times: by France, Italy and Britain, before being ceded to Greece in 1864. Napoleon saw it as the keystone to an Empire in the East. Italy left the architecture of Corfu town, 'all Venetian blue and gold'. Britain left the University of Corfu, good roads and a proper water supply – in the 1930s 'an English house' meant one with a lavatory, commanding twice the rent. Overall, remarks one of Durrell's friends, 'of the vanished Imperial culture of England little remains . . . but . . . cricket lives on independently as the patron saint'.

The legacies of colonial rule lie at the heart of *Bitter Lemons* (1957).

I have a dim memory of the cover of *Prospero's Cell*, perhaps a mysterious green. But to this day I can remember the impact of the bold black outlines and acid lemon-yellow of that Sixties Faber edition. Now published as *Bitter Lemons of Cyprus*, it is a book no less lyrical and exact in its descriptive writing but which offers more of a narrative.

By 1953, when it opens, with a magical voyage from Venice, it seems that Durrell and his wife have separated. With very little money, he settles into lodgings with a Greek schoolmaster, overlooking the harbour of Kyrenia, then buys a little house in a mountain village. Over the three years of his stay on the island he is visited by his small daughter, whom he teaches Greek; by his effervescent mother; and later by his brother Gerald, who arrives with a great deal of equipment. Knowing that 'the minute he started collecting the whole place would be alive with lizards, rats, snakes and every foul creeping thing', Durrell moves out for a while.

There are letters from Henry Miller in Paris; there are other tremendous visitors – Paddy Leigh Fermor and Freya Stark in his first autumn – as well as the new friends Durrell makes wherever he goes: artists, journalists and teachers. And he penetrates the working life of the island, observing it not only as diarist and writer but as publicist for a wine company; English teacher in the Nicosia Gymnasium; and finally as Press Adviser to the Colonial Secretary, at a time when political discontent is rumbling towards violent revolution.

'Journeys, like artists, are born, and not made,' he writes as he sets sail for Cyprus. 'They flower spontaneously out of the demands of our natures – and the best of them lead us not only outwards in space but inwards as well . . . These thoughts belong to Venice at dawn . . . [With the approach of night] we had become once more aware of loneliness and time – those two companions without whom no journey can yield anything.'

Durrell is scholar, philosopher, colourist. His writing is lush and intense. With the dramatic arrival of spring rain, 'Thunder clamoured and rolled, and the grape-blue semi-darkness of the sea was bitten out in magnesium flashes as the lightning clawed at us from Turkey like a family of dragons.'

There are huge contrasts between the beauty of the place and its impoverished, crumbling infrastructure, and between the extremes of feeling about the English. His students at the Gymnasium are in love both with Byron's legendary, heroic death and with Durrell himself – 'I dote my English teacher' – but they drape the blackboard with black crêpe on the anniversary of Greek Independence Day.

Some of the young men in these classes will become recruits to EOKA, the resistance movement formed in 1955 to end British rule and annex the island to Greece. Some will die for it. By the end of the book, the slogans scrawled on whitewashed village walls – THE BRITISH MUST GO . . . WE WILL SHED BLOOD – have given way to bombings. And Durrell himself has at least one attempt made on his life. It is time to go. 'My footsteps echoed softly upon the sea-wall. I was, I realized, very tired after this two years' spell as a servant of the Crown; and I had achieved nothing. It was good to be leaving.'

By the time we three girls arrived in Corfu, Cyprus had been an independent state for five years. Back in ordinary old Surrey, I spent long afternoons in the town bookshop, furtively reading Henry Miller's extraordinary letters to Durrell, all drink and literature and astonishing sex. I had, finally, been abroad, and my mind had been lit: by Mediterranean sun, by my first romance, and by Durrell's deep love-affair with Greece. Perhaps, like him, I had begun to discover myself.

SUE GEE makes a kind of peace with Surrey in her latest novel, *Coming Home*, now out in paperback.

Too Hot to Handle

CHRISTIAN TYLER

It wasn't until the Beijing massacre in June 1989 that I really began to understand what democracy means.

At school we learned about the birth of democracy in ancient Athens; as a teenager I read about Stalin's show trials; as an adult I saw repressive regimes in Eastern Europe and the Soviet Union at first hand. Reporting on the political scene in Britain during the later stages of the Cold War, I heard the words 'freedom' and 'democracy' liberally bandied about; yet they remained for me essentially political slogans.

China was a different matter. I had got to know something of the country in the six years before the 1989 Tiananmen Square sit-in. So the leadership's decision to call in the army, and the subsequent random shooting of hundreds – perhaps thousands – of civilians, I found particularly shocking.

What drove the lesson home for me, however, was the extraordinary testament of one political prisoner, Wei Jingsheng, a pioneer of China's democracy movement. The letters and essays he wrote between 1981 and 1993 during his first, long spell in jail were published in 1997 as *The Courage to Stand Alone.* The book received rave reviews in the West, but Wei was not around to hear the plaudits. He was back in jail.

The letters do not merely prescribe what a democratic China

Wei Jingsheng, *The Courage to Stand Alone: Letters from Prison and Other Writings* (1998, ed. & trans. Kristina M. Torgeson)
Penguin USA · Pb · 284pp · $16 · ISBN 9780140275353

should look like. They convey, in a way no political treatise ever could, what it feels like to live under a regime that has total and arbitrary power over its citizens. The reader shares the impotence of the prisoner silenced for thinking aloud, banished to the outer darkness for challenging the legitimacy of the rulers.

Like Primo Levi, the poet of Auschwitz, Wei reminds us that the human spirit can survive even the most degrading attempts to crush it. He shows, furthermore, that sometimes a single, determined spirit can defeat an entire state. As he writes in a preface: 'Your having this book before you proves the weakness of any powerful dictatorship.'

I wouldn't say that Wei's letters are great literature. They are not graphic like Zhang Xianliang's *Grass Soup*, a gripping account of life in a Chinese labour camp during the great famine of 1958–60. They are not, so far as one can tell from the English translation, particularly stylish. Wei doesn't speak with the same sophistication as his fellow essayist, the academic Liu Xiaobo, a Nobel Peace Prize laureate currently serving an 11-year jail sentence for 'incitement to subvert state power'. The power of Wei's writings lies in their genesis, in the dark and dreadful place from which they come. Their author was cut off from the world, like a frog in a well as Liu Xiaobo puts it, spending years on end in solitary confinement, denied newspapers, books, radio and TV, allowed family visits only infrequently, persecuted round the clock by 'trusties', enduring sleepless nights under glaring lights and insistent noise, suffering from cold, hunger and heart disease, dizzy and sick, while his gums rotted and his teeth fell out. Wei supposed the regime was hoping he would die a 'natural' death, so they couldn't be accused of killing him. But by the time he had come close to death, the world was on his side, and the regime had no choice but to let him out.

The letters, addressed to his family, the prison authorities and senior leaders of the Chinese Communist Party, were partly an antidote to suffering and despair. But Wei also wanted to work out for himself why the Utopian vision of a socialist China had gone so horribly awry and where the responsibility for that lay. He had little contact with Western ideas, and had to start from scratch. Raised on a strict diet of Marxist-Leninist-Mao Zedong Thought, he was an ardent revolutionary, an active Red Guard during the Cultural Revolution, and a soldier in the People's Revolutionary Army. On his travels into the western hinterland of China during that chaotic time, he was shocked by the poverty of the people – the naked, mud-covered children begging by the railway track in Gansu province – by the cruel revenge exacted on so-called 'rightists' exiled to Xinjiang, and the rumours of cannibalism in Ningxia.

The Cultural Revolution had one good thing in its favour. With all the schools shut, there was space and time for a new generation of intellectually curious young Chinese like Wei to rethink their world from the inside out.

We would not have had these letters at all but for a courageous bluff by their author. Apart from those to his brother and sisters, few of them would have got past the censor. But Wei kept copies. He was nearing the end of his first, 15-year sentence in September 1993, when he was suddenly granted parole. It was nine days before the International Olympic Committee was due to vote on China's first bid to host the Olympic Games (those of 2000). Realizing that he'd become a pawn in what he later called a 'dirty and abnormal' game, he played his own move and refused to leave the prison without his copies. They became, he says, the only written denunciation of the Communist leadership to have left a Chinese prison through the front gate.

The bad smell left by the Beijing massacre was still wafting round the world, and China lost the IOC vote by a narrow margin. So, after six months of freedom during which he cheerfully ignored the conditions of his probation, giving interviews to foreign journalists and money to families of the massacre victims, Wei was rearrested, tried and sentenced to a further fourteen years. Now he was the most famous dissident in China. Three and a half years later, as the pressure of world opinion mounted, he was whisked to the airport and put on a plane to Chicago. Friends in the US had meanwhile organized publication of a book containing a selection of his letters and other writings. Wei's first sight of it was when a passenger on the same flight to Chicago asked him to sign his copy.

The published letters are an elaboration of ideas contained in the two documents which made Wei famous, and which led to his arrest. One was a poster calling on the supreme leader Deng Xiaoping to add to his 'Four Modernizations' – science, agriculture, industry and defence – a fifth, democracy. This was dashed off in one night and pasted on Democracy Wall on Beijing's main boulevard in the early hours of 5 December 1978. The other, headed 'Do we want democracy or a new autocracy?' was a response to Deng's crackdown in March the following year and criticized the supreme leader by name.

Their 28-year-old author was working at the time as an electrician at the Beijing zoo, a job assigned to him, as most jobs were in those days. He knew his posters would get him into trouble, but instead of running for the hills he stayed to face arrest. Declaring himself to be no lawbreaker and opposed to violent revolution, he offered himself as a scapegoat – 'the chicken killed as a warning to the monkeys'.

A summary of Wei's political message would look something like this: civil rights are human rights, and there can be no derogation from this universal principle. China's constitution is not worth the paper it is written on because the rights it guarantees are not supported by the law. The law itself is not wielded as an instrument of justice, but as a 'weapon' in the hands of the leadership. The regime is illegitimate as well as inhumane. Everything in China has been reduced to the politics of power, stifling progress in the arts and science. Class struggle is an artificial device to deflect people's anger from Party leaders, and set them at each other's throats. As for China's restless ethnic minorities, all they need is the vote. (Wei took a special interest in the problem of Tibet. His fiancée Ping Ni was Tibetan, the daughter of a former Party boss in the region. He had to give her –

and his chances of a family – up when he was jailed.)

In the letters, the leaders are addressed as equals, or even as inferiors. The tone is by turns serious, humorous, ironic and angry. The bosses are 'old bumpkins who know nothing about economics'; 'this incompetent generation of headstrong old men who think they are omnipotent'. Wei is mischievously familiar with Deng, whom he suspected of personally ordering his arrest and sentence, and whom he accuses of selfish inconsistency. 'We know each other well,' he writes. 'You have great ambition but you're untalented and small-minded.' To others he is more lenient: he signs himself 'Your devoted hostile element' in a letter to the reformist general secretary Hu Yaobang, who was purged in 1987 and whose sudden death in 1989 was one of the causes of the student occupation of Tiananmen Square. He sympathizes with the impotence of Hu's successor, Zhao Ziyang, who opposed sending in the tanks and was put under house arrest until his death in 2005. Wei reserves his deepest scorn for hardliners like premier Li Peng, president Li Xiannian and Party boss Jiang Zemin.

What makes a man capable of sacrificing everything for a principle? Even as a child, Wei could never take no for an answer. 'As a small boy I had always tried to do what others thought was impossible,' he writes. 'If I'm going to do something, I persist to the end. That's the way I am.' He has a self-confidence bordering on arrogance, yet no grand ambition, an almost limitless capacity for suffering and a will of iron which will not allow him to defer, concede or beg. Such was his obduracy, his jailers feared the consequences for themselves. 'You can build walls to contain a man's physical freedom,' Wei writes in a prefatory note, 'but you can never contain his freedom to think. You can never tear down the Democracy Wall in people's hearts.'

One feels almost sorry for the authorities. Wei wouldn't recant, he wouldn't die and they did not dare to kill him. His fame spread, and he became too hot to handle. Like that other dissident Ai Weiwei, well known in the West, he made his resistance into a kind of performance art. And in the end it was the mighty Communist Party, not the prisoner, who proved impotent.

I met Wei once, in 2008. He was 58 and showed no sign of his long ordeal. The ironic sense of humour was very much in evidence. He had come to London to meet politicians, civil servants and academics (none of whom would be photographed with him) because China was preparing to host its first Olympic Games. He told me he was convinced that the Chinese Communist Party was living on borrowed time, and could collapse at any minute. When I accused him of wishful thinking, he laughed. 'It's not just me who says it. The Party thinks the same.'

Wei may be obstinate, but he is not narrow-minded: he takes an interest in the arts and literature, philosophy and scientific invention. He told me that for recreation he goes shooting pheasants in Virginia. Yet dissidents are a special breed. They have a crazy kind of courage, a shocking disregard for their own safety (and, one could say, that of their families). In the Soviet Union they used to be treated as insane and locked up in lunatic asylums. In Mao's China they were beaten and browbeaten until they 'confessed'. These days, they are more likely to be charged with tax evasion.

If dissidents are foolish, then they are holy fools, visionaries who change the course of history like the three with whom Wei has been compared: Nelson Mandela, Vaclav Havel and Andrei Sakharov. I don't mind betting that when the history of post-Communist China comes to be written, the name of the electrician Wei Jingsheng will be up there in lights.

CHRISTIAN TYLER is a former *Financial Times* journalist and the author of *Wild West China: The Taming of Xinjiang*.

Why Must She Grow up?

ROBIN BLAKE

When Richard Hughes looked back at how he wrote his first and most successful novel, he described the process rather beguilingly. In 1926, when he was 26, he retired for the winter 'to the little Adriatic island town of Capodistria, where the exchange was then so favourable that I could live on next to nothing – which is all I had – and where the only language spoken was Italian, of which (at first at any rate) I knew not a word, so that I could work all day in the Café della Loggia undisturbed by the chatter'. He wrote in this semi-operatic self-exile with such meticulous care that just one chapter was completed before his winter was over. 'This may seem slow going but I had decided my book was to be a short one and it is always what a writer leaves out of his book, not what he puts in, that takes the time.'

The book was *A High Wind in Jamaica* (1929) and it is indeed a short book, but one that grips and fizzes with ideas, images and energy. Thirty-five years ago, as an inexperienced schoolteacher, I had the task of interesting a class of 16-year-olds in it, and I thought it would be ideal fare for them. Set around the middle of the nineteenth century, the novel takes the outward form of an adventure story. The ingredients are a group of children and their life on a decayed plantation, then an earthquake, a hurricane, a sailing ship, the high seas, the capture of the children by pirates and a final rescue and return to normality in England. The passing incidents include some farcical goings-on with pirates dressed as women, a ludicrous

---

Richard Hughes, *A High Wind in Jamaica* (1929)
Vintage · Pb · 192pp · £7.99 · ISBN 9780099437437

quayside auction of the pirates' booty, some uproarious banqueting, a fight between a goat and a pig, another between a tiger and a lion – or an attempt to stage one – and a chase after a drunken monkey in the ship's rigging. So far, so *Pirates of the Caribbean*; but there is also a dark side: the shocking accidental death of a child, a murder, a fatal betrayal and a hanging.

A High Wind in Jamaica has often been compared to William Golding's *Lord of the Flies* in that both stories take as their starting-point popular nineteenth-century children's tales and give a twist to their basic premises: Golding, writing in the early 1950s, destroyed the noble innocence of R. M. Ballantyne's young protagonists in *Coral Island* while, almost thirty years earlier, Hughes's had taken another famous juvenile adventure, *Treasure Island*, and daringly re-imagined it as a study of the mystery of the child-psyche at the approach of puberty.

To my surprise the teenagers in my class were underwhelmed by the book, and many hated it altogether. I puzzled over this. Perhaps it was that most teenagers, having recently left childhood behind, didn't appreciate having to dwell on it again, whatever the context. Moreover the children in this story appear decidedly odd. Events are largely seen through the haunted eyes of 10-year-old Emily who, by contrast with most children in fiction, is complex, egotistical, hyper-sensitive and far from innocent. Wary in general of moral ambiguity, my pupils found they didn't like her, and would have preferred a more sympathetic central character, whom they could root or feel sorry for – Ralph in *Lord of the Flies* fitted the bill or, in another stalwart of the O-level curriculum, Snowball in *Animal Farm*.

The students' thumbs-down to the book might have been attributable to my falling short as a teacher, but there is a much more serious problem about *A High Wind in Jamaica* as a schoolroom text, which has now (as far as I know) resulted in its permanent banishment from the GCSE curriculum. Though there are three boys in *A High Wind*'s cast, Hughes is hardly interested in them as characters.

All his concentration is on young Emily and (to a lesser extent) the other girls, Margaret, Rachel and Laura. For a man to write a story about female children from, as it were, the inside cannot in itself be held against him. But Hughes takes the extraordinary risk of introducing sex into the project. It is not explicit, yet it hovers fitfully, like a spectre, over the future of the young hostages. Margaret is 13 and becoming sexually aware. Soon after being taken aboard the pirate ship she leaves the children's accommodation to sleep in the cabin and to spend all her time with the pirates. Her absence is not interpreted, but it subtly changes the atmosphere of the story in a way that the reader knows can never be reversed.

Then there are the equally touchy questions of slavery and race. When taken hostage by the pirates, the children are passengers to England from Jamaica, where their homes have been flattened by the aforementioned hurricane. Emily and her siblings had lived on an old sugar estate, not worked since the (relatively recent) emancipation of the slaves. That is the background to the thoughts that come to her in the immediate aftermath of the storm:

> It was not the hurricane she was thinking of, it was the death of Tabby. That, at times, seemed a horror beyond all bearing. It was her first intimate contact with death – and a death of violence, too. The death of Old Sam had no such effect: there is, after all, a vast difference between a negro and a favourite cat.

Such words in print must shock to the bone anyone in education today. You could say, as I myself did in the 1970s, no matter: the challenge is an educational one. You have to explore Hughes's words in context – their dramatic irony, the fact that they are the callous thoughts of a child – and you should also take a historical perspective: just because something is unthinkable now does not mean it was not, once, as thinkable to some people as hopscotch or lemon pie. But what if an anti-racist parent should read this passage? What if it were taken up by racist children in the school playground? Books have been removed from library shelves for containing less incendiary statements. Far better to avoid these confrontations.

There is no doubt that the long-term careers of certain books can be blighted if educators take against them. While *Animal Farm*'s stock has risen ever higher, and *Lord of the Flies* has never dropped out of print, *A High Wind* has shifted uneasily (and I suppose unprofitably) around the publishing map as successive publishers have reissued it and then let it fall out of print. Yet the book is a master class in how to tell a story – emotionally oblique and happy to leave its readers to do a good deal of interpretive work for themselves, and at the same time exceptionally alert to imagery, characterization, literary irony and moral subtext. That makes it sound like a dutiful series of Lit. Crit. boxes ticked. But re-reading it after more than three decades I found that *A High Wind* brings all its ingredients together like a perfectly cooked meal to present a tale full of texture and tastes. It is immensely satisfying. For a starter we have the compelling set-piece description of the hurricane in the section said by the author to have been the sole product of his stay in Capodistria.

> The negro huts were clean gone, and the negroes crawling on their stomachs across the compound to gain the shelter of the house. The bouncing rain seemed to cover the ground with a white smoke, a sort of sea in which the blacks wallowed like porpoises. One nigger-boy began to roll away: his mother, forgetting caution, rose to her feet: and immediately the fat old beldam was blown clean away, bowling along across the fields and hedgerows like someone in a funny fairy story, till she fetched up against a wall and was pinned there, unable to move.

The rest of Hughes's meal is served up with equal panache and conviction. A great part of his attraction as a narrator is that he *knows things*. He can describe what it is like to encounter an octopus when diving, or to stand above a beach and witness the proximate effects of a deep-sea earthquake. He understands the nature of a sea-going schooner to be 'one of the most mechanically satisfactory, austere, unornamented engines ever invented by Man'. He knows the effect of seasickness on a lion, the capabilities of a monkey under the influence of rum, how to make 'that potion known in alcoholic circles as Hangman's Blood'.

Anna Trench

There are times, after the tumultuous opening, when the narrative slows down, and nothing much appears to be happening. In fact things are happening but the adults are out of sight, or on the periphery, while the children are left to discover the pleasures of life on a sailing vessel.

> The most lasting joy undoubtedly lay in that network of footropes and chains and stays that spreads out under and on each side of the bowsprit. Here familiarity only bred content. Here, in fine weather, one could climb or be still: stand, sit, hang, swing or lie: now this end up, now that: and all with the cream of the blue sea being whipt up for one's own special pleasure, almost within touching distance.

This is prose under perfect cadenced control. It sometimes rises very near poetry:

> The schooner moved just enough for the sea to divide with a slight rustle on her stem, breaking out into a shower of sparks, which lit up also wherever the water rubbed the ship's side, as if the ocean were a tissue of sensitive nerves; and still twinkled behind in the paleness of the wake.

The narrative never stands still for long, however, and when the end approaches it comes quickly, and with brutal finality for the pirates. As they stand trial at the Old Bailey – not merely for piracy but for a murder they did not commit – Hughes nicely conveys the curious atmosphere of a criminal courtroom, and just how a judge might seem to an imaginative child witness (Emily, in fact): 'dressed in his strange disguise, toying with a pretty nosegay, he looked like some benign old wizard who spent his magic in doing good'.

When the trial is over Emily still doesn't acknowledge what she has been involved in, and asks her father, 'What was it all about? Why did I have to learn all those questions?' But it is those questions, or rather the answers that Emily has been coached to learn by heart, that write the death warrant for the pirate captain Olson, Otto his mate, and the rest.

Emily is far from stupid and by no means incapable of understanding the fatal role she has played in the trial. She simply suppresses the knowledge. Much earlier on, while still aboard Jonsen's schooner, a wave of self-consciousness suddenly breaks over her and she cries out to herself (in an echo of another child involved with pirates), 'Oh, why must she grow up?' Many novelists would wrap up such a story with the conclusion that Emily, after all her extraordinary experiences, *has* grown up. But this is not Richard Hughes's conception of Emily. She may know she will, she must, become an adult – but slyly, and protected by a cloak of false innocence, she will put off reaching that crux of responsibility, and will do so for as long as she possibly can.

The account by Hughes of his visit to Capodistria in 1926 omits at least one significant fact: he had gone abroad in full flight from a callow and disastrous sexual affair. Perhaps that is the hidden key to this great book's bittersweet and, I think, tragic view of the life of a child – a life inescapably innocent and guilty, outgoing and self-absorbed, clung-to and betrayed.

ROBIN BLAKE's third novel about the Georgian coroner of Preston, Titus Cragg, will be published in the New Year. He lives partly in London and partly in the eighteenth century.

The Most Precious Book I Own

ADAM FOULDS

I am not a book collector and I'm not fussy about particular editions. As long as the words are there I don't mind. Deciding on an especially precious book, I first considered something I received as a school prize, the Macmillan edition of Yeats's *Collected Poems*. That book was a magical object for me as a teenager. I was for some time obsessed with the melodies of Yeats's early poems and moved by their forthright, challenging pathos: 'Tread softly because you tread on my dreams' or

> I must be gone: there is a grave
> Where daffodil and lily wave . . .

There was an intricate Celtic design in gold on the bright green cover, and on the back was Yeats's face, with dream-heavy eyelids, as painted by Augustus John. It was a portal, that book, but even so it was replaceable and it's no longer the edition I read.

There is only one book I own that I know I will always want to keep. It's small and unprepossessing, navy blue, about five inches by three, and is inscribed 'Pte I. Masidlover', who was my grandfather. *A Book of Jewish Thoughts*, selected by the Chief Rabbi Dr Hertz, was issued in 1942 to 'His Majesty's Jewish sailors, soldiers and airmen'. My copy also bears the stamp of another excellent name, Rabbi Dayan M. Gollop, Senior Jewish Chaplain to HM Forces. The book's size means, I suppose, that it could be kept buttoned into a top pocket and taken anywhere.

The quotations in the book come from a range of sacred texts, commentaries and later authors, among them Einstein, Winston

Churchill and Franklin D. Roosevelt. They are arranged by subject, beginning, with pleasing archaic resonance, 'I Am an Hebrew', and ending with meditations on 'Time and Eternity'. Various moments of Jewish history are invoked. Ephraim of Bonn, writing in 1180 about the Second Crusade, praises Bernard of Clairvaux for bringing a halt to violence towards Jews. Elsewhere an early twentieth-century pogrom is recalled. There is evidently good reason for the patriotic fervour of a poem called *The Jewish Soldier*:

> Thou hast given us home and freedom, Mother England,
> Thou hast let us live again,
> Free and fearless, 'midst thy free and fearless children . . .

This little object is saturated with its historical moment. I read it wondering what was known about what was happening at the time and all the places copies of this book went. Anti-Semitism is decried by Tolstoy and others, and the German horror alluded to (Einstein protests against the racial laws imposed on German universities), although none of its authors or readers could have known what we know now. The book tries to fortify its readers with a celebration of the depth and resilience of Jewish culture. The selection distils from scripture the essence of Jewish theological and moral vision. It does this, I think, very well. I certainly recognize the emphasis on free will, moral choice and personal agency, that exhortation to take your place in the world as an upright, three-dimensional, adult human being that reflects Judaism's 'high estimate of man', to use a phrase of Maxim Gorky's quoted in the section 'The Testimony of the Nations'.

Finally, it offers faith and stoicism in the face of adversity and death. I am not religious but I think that if I were going out to meet those things I might well put it in my top pocket. I'd have my grandfather with me at any rate.

ADAM FOULDS's new novel, *In the Wolf's Mouth*, has just been published. This article was commissioned in conjunction with the Royal Society of Literature's *Review*.

Hound Dogs

ANTHONY GARDNER

When I was 18 I travelled around America by Greyhound bus. I still have the Hagstrom folding map I took with me, my gap-year odyssey marked out in black felt-tip pen: west from New York, skirting the Great Lakes; across the vast prairies of Minnesota and North Dakota; over the Rockies to Salt Lake City and San Francisco; back through Arizona, Texas and the Deep South. It was the first great adventure of my life – one that has yet to be surpassed.

My perception of Greyhounds was a romantic one, based on the song that inspired my journey: Paul Simon's 'America'. But in the years that followed I found surprisingly few references to them in popular culture. And not until I was asked to review Irma Kurtz's *The Great American Bus Ride* (1993) did I come across a book that did justice to the extraordinary experience they offered.

Because Irma Kurtz was best known as the agony aunt for *Cosmopolitan*, I snootily assumed that she couldn't be much of a writer. I soon realized my mistake. From the outset she proved the most engaging of companions: wise, compassionate and witty, with a beautiful turn of phrase, an excellent ear for dialogue, and a fine line in self-deprecation: 'The truth is, I am a hussy of low appetites who always yearns shamelessly for rough travel, and I grab the chance whenever I can to arrive at my destination exhausted, knowing I've earned my goal the hard way. Greyhound and I were made for each other.'

To European eyes, Greyhound's Americruisers with their red,

Irma Kurtz, *The Great American Bus Ride* (1993), is out of print.

white and blue livery look glamorous, even luxurious. But as Kurtz makes clear, no one in the automobile-obsessed USA takes the bus if they can help it. It is the preserve of the young, those down on their luck, and the mad; Greyhound depots, generally in the dodgiest part of town, are modern-day last-chance saloons. Yet for anyone keen to understand the country's immensity and variety, there is no better form of transport.

Though Kurtz travelled, as I did, from New York to California and back, her journey had a very different impetus to mine. American-born, she had lived as an expatriate for more than thirty years when she decided in her mid-fifties to explore 'that most baffling of all places, my unknown homeland'. The stopping-points were chosen partly in homage to family history – her mother's childhood home in Indiana; a favourite holiday resort in Florida – and partly on a whim. Fargo in North Dakota seemed a must 'simply because I thought it was one of the least likely places in which I could ever find myself'.

As both a native and a stranger, she is able to sketch the continent's cities and landscape with a rare degree of understanding and objectivity. Imagining New York through the eyes of the Russian babushka next to her, she sees 'Words, words, words, everywhere high and low. Words in neon waiting to blaze, words embossed, hand-painted . . . warnings, descriptions, names, jokes, enticements, profanities. In Moscow there is stone-gray visual silence everywhere; she must have been deafened by Manhattan.' Crossing the plains of Oklahoma, Kurtz finds an epic quality in their flatness, such as the first pioneers must have wondered at:

> It was bewitching and wild. Set anything rolling out there on the flat – a barrel of beer, a wagon wheel, an idea – and it'll be bound to travel all the way around the world and come back from behind you. The way that state is made, when a Kansas mother sees her child off into adventures, she has to stand at her front door waving goodbye until nightfall. They say when

> the twisters blow over Kansas, with nothing in their way to stop them, they pick their way as daintily as geisha girls.

At the heart of the book, however, are the buses themselves: 'the state without a zip code, the great moving community that is Greyhound USA'. The onboard geography never varies: the coveted front seats go to the old and infirm, or those so cantankerous that no one dares argue with them; the next dozen rows accommodate the more genteel passengers; the back is where the bad boys congregate. Men instinctively sit next to men, women next to women, whites next to whites, and so on. But each Greyhound has its own identity, determined by its driver, route and passengers. The bus Kurtz joins in St Louis is a party, noisy with gleeful running jokes; LA to Las Vegas is the gamblers' express, on which a 10-year-old fleeces her grandmother at gin rummy.

Footloose though Kurtz's fellow-travellers are, few of them have any sense of the world beyond their homeland. 'Are you a missionary?' asks one on learning that Kurtz lives in England – and in some respects she is. While she only once confesses to being an agony aunt, her book could have been entitled *Busman's Holiday*, so anxious are strangers to pour out their hearts to her. The parade of garrulous oddballs whose conversations she records becomes addictively fascinating. No sooner has she shaken off Vera – a troubled, oversized nurse from 'an age when doorways were cast out of boulders' – than she is buttonholed by a reformed alcoholic whose girlfriend has just drunk herself to death. Exhausted, Kurtz places herself next to someone she is quite sure will spare her his confidences, a quiet young Vietnamese. But no: she only has to glance at him to set him off.

> 'My mom kicked me out last night in Seattle,' he said. 'I'm 23 years old and we've been in this country since I was seven, and she still treats me like a baby. Is that right? It is not the American way. Well, I've had all I can take . . .'

Among these glimpses of other lives are moments of deep pathos and despair. A little Amish girl brightens at the sight of a red ball, only to be re-enveloped by her solemn family; a beautiful, abused dancer becomes a ghost of herself as a sinister older man steps forward to meet her. But other encounters are life-affirming: a Japanese boy tends his frail grandfather with touching devotion; an apparently mismatched hobo couple prove on closer acquaintance to be 'great and true lovers'. And Kurtz never loses her good humour for long, for at every stop there is the thrill of boarding a bus for a new destination: 'a moment of the pure delight that gulls must feel when they trust their wings to the prevailing breeze'.

The book is littered with wonderful throw-away lines, engaging metaphors and polished aphorisms. Of a needy divorcée: 'She was entering the time of life when friends, and enemies, start to say what a fine-looking woman she used to be.' Of Spanish-speaking passengers in California: 'their rapid exchanges flew like freshly milled pepper, and spiced the air for our entry into San Francisco'. A Mormon film about the Nativity is so preposterous that 'even the sheep cast incredulous looks at the camera'; a cemetery in New England is inhabited by feral cats, 'descended perhaps from familiars that fled north three hundred years ago when things got too hot for them in Salem'.

Kurtz's narrative barely touches on her upbringing in America, but central to her quest is a grandfather she never knew. Behind a shopping centre in Denver she finds the remains of the sanatorium where he died of tuberculosis seventy-five years before, and to which her grandmother gave his beautifully bound set of the *Jewish Encyclopaedia*. The building is now a cancer-research centre; the old library has long since been dismantled. But a sympathetic stranger suggests that she try the administrator's office.

> Behind a dignified desk, shelves reached nearly to the ceiling, and distributed on them were old books, all substantially

bound. End to end, on the very top shelf, was a set of volumes in dark blue, lettered in gold. My guide fetched down the first in the row and gave it to me; it fell open in my hands. Ornately scrolled and bordered in front of me was my grandfather's ex libris . . . [I] looked at my friend. His eyes were glowing; he'd shed years. My grandfather had entered his history too, and would ever be a part of him, as he was of me.

From time to time over the past three decades I have thought of retracing my journey through the States. Now that I have reached the age at which Irma Kurtz set out, I am filled with new admiration for her enterprise, and wonder whether I too would still have the resilience to face eight-hour bus rides and deserted midnight depots. But if anything could persuade me to reach for my rucksack again, it would be this book, with its unflagging sense of adventure and delight in the open road.

ANTHONY GARDNER is often to be found on the No.52 bus to Notting Hill, though he wishes that its route didn't include that irritating detour to the Ladbroke Grove Sainsbury's. He edits the Royal Society of Literature's *Review* and is working on a novel which may include a journey by Greyhound.

Anna Trench

A Scientist for All Seasons

CATHERINE MERRICK

Edward O. Wilson, naturalist, theorist and Harvard Professor of Entomology, will be 85 this year: he is showing little sign of slowing down. In an eminent and eclectic career spanning six decades he has become one of the most eloquent public figures in modern science, produced an impressive collection of books, both scholarly and general, and won two Pulitzer Prizes for non-fiction. Most recently, aged 80, he produced his first novel. 'He is', says Richard Dawkins, 'hugely learned, not just in his field of social insects, but in anthropology and other subjects as well. He is an outstanding synthesizer, his knowledge is immense and he manages to bring it all together in a coherent way.'

This talent for synthesis is fully displayed in Wilson's most enduring and influential theory, which first appeared in 1984 with his book *Biophilia*. Wilson coined the term 'biophilia' to describe what he believes is an innate human affinity with other forms of life. It is innate because our culture and behaviour are partially encoded in our genes, and it has been sustained throughout evolution because human life and death have always depended primarily upon our fellow creatures.

Put simply, we are hard-wired to be interested in living things. *Biophilia* provides some fascinating evidence for this idea, along with the author's engaging and erudite reflections on what such a human instinct might mean for life on earth. To Wilson, it means that we are

---

E. O. Wilson, *Biophilia* (1984)
Harvard University Press · Pb · 176pp · £18.95 · ISBN 9780674074422

naturalists by nature: an instinct that can and should be exploited to promote conservation.

Indeed, Professor Wilson is himself a passionate conservation advocate. In the past thirty years, he has followed his seminal book with *The Diversity of Life* (1992), *The Biophilia Hypothesis* (1993), *The Future of Life* (2003) and, most recently, *The Creation: An Appeal to Save Life on Earth* (2006). The growing grandeur of these titles reflects not only their author's increasing stature but also his growing sense of urgency. When I heard him give the Prather Lectures at Harvard in 2010, he was very much in environmental advocacy mode, energetically pacing the podium although his tall frame is now stooped and his deep Southern drawl quavers with age. Scientists are a contrarian lot, not much given to hero-worship, yet in a lecture hall packed with young biologists, the sense of being in the presence of greatness was palpable.

In fact, it is as a writer rather than a lecturer that E. O. Wilson has been most honoured, and justly so. 'The ideal scientist', he states in *Biophilia*, 'can be said to think like a poet, work like a clerk, and write like a journalist.' For Ian McEwan, who has cited Wilson as an intellectual hero, the professor certainly embodies his own ideal: 'I do not know of another working scientist whose prose is better than his. He can be witty, scathing and inspirational by turns.' Unlike McEwan, Wilson may not be a great writer of fiction (his recent novel, *Anthill*, received mixed reviews). He is, however, indubitably a great writer of science. *Biophilia*, which focuses entirely on his personal scientific passions, shows him at his authorial best: the book is poetic, discursive, highly readable and still relevant.

Wilson writes from the heart here: he is keenly aware of his own biophilia. He begins and ends with eloquent passages describing the forests of Surinam, where he experienced an epiphany as a young scientist doing fieldwork on ants:

> At Bernhardsdorp I imagined the richness and order as an

> intensity of light. The woman, child and peccary turned into incandescent points. Around them the village became a black disk, relatively devoid of life, its artefacts adding next to nothing. The woodland beyond was a luminous bank, sparked here and there by moving lights of birds, mammals and larger insects.

From this moment of inspiration, Wilson expands on his theory in a series of loosely linked essays discussing the evidence for human biophilia as a genetically encoded instinct. The idea that our behaviour is to some extent genetic was a natural, yet audacious, extension of his academic work on social insects, in which a set of inborn instincts can create a society whose sophistication far exceeds the processing power of a single ant or bee. Could the same be true of humans, wondered Wilson? Do we, unlike ants, learn our culture *de novo* from birth, or are we also to some extent born with it?

This idea, which eventually gave rise to the whole modern discipline of evolutionary psychology, got Wilson into very hot water when he first published it in *Sociobiology: The New Synthesis* in 1975. Nature versus nurture may be an old debate now, but it was political dynamite in the 1970s. Anthropologists and sociologists saw Wilson's book as a dangerous attack on the uniqueness of human nature; he was accused of genetic determinism, racism, misogyny. An anti-racism activist famously emptied a jug of water over him at a scientific conference. 'I believe', he said later, with pride, 'that I was the only scientist in modern times to be physically attacked for an idea.'

Undeterred by such controversy, Wilson went on to produce *Biophilia*, making a persuasive case for the role of 'nature' when it comes to our engagement with the living world. Humans, for example, tend to be both fascinated by and afraid of snakes, as indeed do apes and monkeys, even those born in laboratories. (Madagascan lemurs, notably, do not: there are no deadly snakes on the island.)

Thus, snakes engender one of our commonest phobias. Why? Because the man most intensely attuned to the sight of a snake was once the man most likely to survive.

> How could it be otherwise? The brain evolved into its present form over a period of about two million years, from the time of *Homo habilis* to the late stone age of *Homo sapiens*, during which people existed in hunter-gatherer bands in intimate contact with the natural environment. Snakes mattered. The smell of water, the hum of a bee, the directional bend of a plant stalk mattered . . . And a sweet sense of horror, the shivery fascination with monsters and creeping forms that so delights us in the sterile hearts of the cities, could see you through to the next morning . . . Although the evidence is far from all in, the brain appears to have kept its old capacities, its channelled quickness. We stay alert and alive in the vanished forests of the world.

Indeed, continues Wilson, it's not only the life that could kill us that retains a genetic footprint in our brains, it is the life that could sustain us too. He suggests that we instinctively attempt to recreate the vanished forests – or, more accurately, the vanished savannah habitats – of early man in our cities. The landscapes that please us tend to feature open grassland, clumps of sheltering trees and running water: city parks from New York to Kyoto look this way. Modern man no longer actually needs these things, but his instincts do not yet know it.

None of this, in Wilson's opinion, diminishes our human nature. His theory is presented as a unifying and inclusive one: biophilia is manifest everywhere from the study of biology to the use of living symbols in art, mythology and faith. Science and art are not opposing forces, but complementary expressions of a central human instinct. Does a scientist's desire to understand a bird of paradise reduce the emotional impact of its beauty? Quite the opposite, says Wilson: the better our understanding, the deeper our aesthetic appreciation of the bird. By the same token, the better we understand our own brains, the more richly we can live within them.

Biophilia is a short book remarkably long on ideas. I would argue that the case it makes for our 'genetic nature' should, if anything, be broader: instincts for non-living forces like astronomy and meteorology should exist alongside our biophilia if human survival once depended on weather or on tides. Indeed, perhaps they *do* exist. Nevertheless, our instinct for the earthly probably outweighs any instinct for the heavenly. In fact, the book takes an unusually sci-fi leap in suggesting that our biophilia may eventually prevent us from colonizing distant planets: their sterile environments would drive us mad. Returning to the here and now, it concludes with a heartfelt chapter advocating the conservation of our own planet: not for future generations or for the sake of idealism, but for our own instinctive satisfaction. It is here that Wilson the pragmatist meets Wilson the idealist, for he is, like most great scientists, both at once. 'What do we really owe our remote descendants? At the risk of offending some readers I will suggest: Nothing. Obligations simply lose their meaning across centuries. But what do we owe ourselves in planning for them? Everything.'

E. O. Wilson is, in the words of his admirer Ian McEwan, 'fundamentally a rational optimist who shows us the beauty of the narrative of life on earth. He is living proof that materialism need not be a bleak world view.' Thus, in an age when environmentalism can seem very bleak indeed, *Biophilia* reads like a breath of fresh air. It is a book to raise your spirits about the nature of humanity, and to offer food for thought for years to come.

CATHERINE MERRICK is a biologist and lecturer at Keele University. She spends much of her time trying to instil a rigorous and pragmatic biophilia in undergraduate biologists.

Mad about the Girl

CONSTANTINE FRASER

On the front cover of my copy of *Zuleika Dobson*, a magnificently dressed young man maintains an impeccable posture as he topples backwards off a barge and into the Isis. As he plunges towards the water, apparently ready to shatter on impact, he gravely doffs his hat to a smiling girl on the deck. This girl, naturally, is Zuleika.

Caricaturist, essayist and dandy, Max Beerbohm only ever wrote one novel. The delicious final product, published in 1911 and subtitled *An Oxford Love Story*, was described as a literary burlesque by H. L. Mencken: not serious enough to be a straightforward fable, it's too gentle in its irony and too politically disengaged to be true satire. Recommended by my grandmother as I was about to start university, my tatty Penguin quickly became a constant companion, sitting on my shelf, following me back to London during vacations and providing me with bedtime reading ever since.

Mary Kuper

Zuleika is an underwhelming professional magician and the granddaughter of the Warden of Judas College; her true talent lies in her infinite sex appeal. By the time her train pulls into Oxford station, she is already 'the toast of two hemi-

---

Max Beerbohm, *Zuleika Dobson* (1911)
Collector's Library · Hb · 288pp · £9.99 · ISBN 9781907360220

spheres', kept in lavish style by legions of besotted admirers ranging in rank from Russian aristocrats (the Grand Duke Salamander Salamandrovitch among them) to anonymous waiters. She can soon add herds of impressionable undergraduates to the list.

But Miss Dobson, for all her mystique, suffers from the familiar human trait of desiring only what she cannot have, and she meets her match in the form of a cold and effortlessly superior aristocrat, the Duke of Dorset. They alternate in pursuit of one another, until their courtship finally culminates in the suicide by drowning of the university's entire undergraduate population in a futile display of adoration, all of which naturally leaves Zuleika feeling rather flattered.

Edwardian Oxford is already a strange enough place to modern eyes, and this resolutely silly plot pushes the novel into the land of affectionate parody. Callow young men are no sooner out of boarding-school than they are cloistered away in colleges; with literature their only guide to women, it's hardly surprising that they deal with Zuleika's arrival by casting themselves as romantic heroes, and her as the incarnation of ideal love. Witness the Duke, having decidedly warmed to her by now:

> 'My heart is a bright hard gem, proof against any die. Came Cupid, with one of his arrow-points for graver, and what he cut on the gem's surface never can be effaced. There, deeply and for ever, your image is intagliated. No years, nor fires, nor cataclysm of total Nature, can erase from that great gem your image.'
>
> 'My dear Duke,' said Zuleika, 'don't be so silly.'

Even the novelist's art, and with it his own writerly ambitions, are targets for Beerbohm's caricature. Every cliché and literary excess makes an appearance, as owls prophesy doom and the narrator invokes the Muses, all in richly purple aestheticist prose.

> The moon, like a gardenia in the night's buttonhole – but no!

> why should a writer never be able to mention the moon without likening her to something else – usually something to which she bears not the faintest resemblance? . . . The moon, looking like nothing whatsoever but herself, was engaged in her old and futile endeavour to mark the hours correctly on the sun-dial at the centre of the lawn . . .

If *Zuleika Dobson* has a major flaw, it is Beerbohm's refusal to take his novel seriously. In the age of hipsters and postmodernism, sophisticated ironic posturing is starting to seem rather *passé*. However, for the modern reader there is a darker and far more poignant irony in the timing of the novel's publication. Beerbohm could not know of the imminent and this time very real destruction of the same young men who potter about blissfully in its pages. Three summers on, and Larkin's 'moustached archaic faces' would still be smiling as they queued outside recruiting offices, unable to grasp that they might now have something worth taking very seriously indeed. With hindsight, *Zuleika*'s silliness and Beerbohm's self-indulgence start to seem more like doomed innocence.

The old train station, which could once 'whisper to the tourist the last enchantments of the Middle Age', has long since been torn down, and Oxford has lost its unhealthily monastic tendencies. But Beerbohm's burlesque remains as enchanting as ever, and he would no doubt have been delighted by *Zuleika*'s 1950s adaptation into that most kitsch of artistic forms, the West End musical.

Not too long ago, when some interview in the Sunday papers prompted me to ponder what items I would save from a house fire, I realized the extent to which Miss Dobson had insinuated herself into my affections. So perhaps it's no surprise that when I eventually found myself packing to move to the other end of Europe, I decided I couldn't very well leave her behind.

CONSTANTINE FRASER fears he might be totally unemployable, and has temporarily postponed his entry into the real world by moving to Athens.

Magic Casements

PENELOPE LIVELY

Francis Spufford's *The Child that Books Built* is a short book that seems long, expansive, excursive. Of course – it cites a host of other books, from *Where the Wild Things Are* through *The Little House on the Prairie* to *Nineteen Eighty-Four*; it is packed with reference, with discussion. A book about books and, above all, a book about the power of books, about the manipulative effect of fiction, about the way in which story can both mirror and influence the process of growing up. A child learns to read, discovers the possibilities of that retreat into the pages of a book, and its life is never quite the same again.

Francis Spufford describes his own childhood reading addiction and, in the process, dissects with wit and erudition the significant forces at work behind fairy story, behind mythology, behind such archetypal story-telling as science fiction, behind the eventual complexity of novelists such as Borges and Calvino. He charts his own reading life, from the moment 'the furze of black marks between the covers of *The Hobbit* grew lucid, and released a dragon' to his adolescent forays into meta-fiction, stories about stories.

What have books done, for the reading child? Spufford is clear: 'They freed us from the limitations of having just one limited life with one point of view; they let us see beyond the horizon of our own circumstances.' Quite so. Reading is not escape – though it can indeed be that too; it is the discovery of alternative existences, where

---

Francis Spufford, *The Child that Books Built* (2002)
Faber · Pb · 224pp · £9.99 · ISBN 9780571214679

things are done differently. It is the discovery of our own disturbing nature, as we see a little boy tame the rampaging, snorting monsters of his own anger in *Where the Wild Things Are*. It is the discovery of the moral obligations of adult society, as we endure *The Long Winter* with Laura and her family in a snow-bound town in Dakota. We are condemned to live one life – as me, myself, in the prison of my own mind; but no, we are not, we discover – through reading we can live many lives, and thus we learn how better to manage our own.

It is a gloriously universal piece of writing. All readers who have themselves been built by books will be nodding in agreement or making further suggestions. My own response when first I read *The Child that Books Built*, I remember, was: why has no one written this book before? But Spufford has written it magisterially, eclectically. I was nodding fervently at his salute to the robust, adult-free world of Arthur Ransome's sailor children, which enthralled me as a 10-year-old in hot, dusty Egypt, reading in wonder of this mythic place of water, greenery and independence. I had to part company with him when it came to his enthusiasm for the Narnia books, which I cannot abide. But of course I never knew them as a child, only met them as an adult and disliked that creepy lion, the Christian message; that perhaps makes all the difference, the reading perspective – child or adult. Though I would certainly contend that if a children's book is any good it must be as readable for an adult as for a child. W. H. Auden put it perfectly: 'There are good books which are only for adults, because their comprehension presupposes adult experiences, but there are no good books which are only for children.'

Anna Trench

Absolutely. Though I would want to make a qualification: some books may serve to introduce adult experience in a way that expands rather than confuses the child's perception of the world. But, centrally, it is the abiding quality of the immortal writing that seizes anyone of any age, which means that for those lavishly supplied with reading matter as children it is the language and images of the greats of children's literature that lodge in the head for ever. Never mind everything that gets shovelled in later, the Cheshire Cat, the Mad Hatter, the Jumblies, the Owl and the Pussycat and so much else will always surface, the essential sediment of a reading lifetime because this was the real thing, the combination of story, originality and imaginative power.

'A memoir of childhood reading', Spufford calls his book, and it is a memoir also of a childhood haunted by the tragedy of his younger sister, Bridget, who suffered from cystinosis – a condition so rare that there were at the time only twenty others with it in Britain. Management of this debilitating illness drained her parents, dominated family life. Her older brother fled into books – in denial, in retreat. At the age of 7 he learnt that Bridget was going to die. He was reading mythology at the time – *The God beneath the Sea* by Leon Garfield and Edward Blishen – and was able to see the savagery of this undeserved verdict as a reflection of the harsh realities of the world of mythology. Terrible things happen to the good just as much as to the bad: misfortune is randomly dealt.

A defining moment for the 7-year-old, which seemed to run parallel with his reading experience. He had been familiar with fairy tales, in which 'character is destiny . . . you can predict what will happen to a good princess, just from the fact that she is a good princess'. Fairy tales are inhabited by types: witches, fairy godmothers, wicked stepmothers. Back in their distant past, they served up hope to a credulous peasantry, for whom not much went right: evil does get its comeuppance, virtue can be rewarded. In the nurseries of the twentieth century they were the archetypal story – this happens because someone did this or that, and the consequence was . . . Or, if you subscribe to the darker theories of Bruno Bettelheim, each tale is a vehicle for the struggle between the id and the ego. I remember being uncomfortably fascinated by Bettelheim when I was a young mother, nervously reading *Little Red Riding Hood* or whatever to the children and hoping their tender minds were not being thrown into turmoil. I am relieved to read that he is somewhat discredited nowadays.

Spufford's analysis of his response to reading is in effect the story of his growing up, of the maturing mind. His intriguing discussion of the moral pointers implicit in Laura Ingalls Wilder's *The Long Winter* demonstrates how 'I learned what people did and did not owe each other'. This story of the inhabitants of a snow-bound town in the nineteenth-century American Midwest, who save themselves and one another when food begins to run out, taught a late-twentieth-century boy the rules of social obligation. He sees the identifying features of children's literature as that essential component of story married with a structure of judgements, the provision of moral experience alongside compelling atmosphere.

And then there comes the dismaying moment when the voracious exploring adolescent reader is impelled to move on – to read wider, further. But where, what? Oh yes, I remember too – that baffled engagement with 'grown-up' books, which were both alluring and often obscure. Spufford compares the relative certainties of children's literature with the deliberate – and desirable – ambiguities of adult fiction. It is a quantum leap for the 15-year-old to take that on. And then there is the question of gender; boys do indeed seek out one thing, girls another. Spufford relished James Bond: Jane Austen did not appeal. He found science fiction, and became an addict. He flirted with pornography – pretty soft porn, by the sound of it, but I am no authority. And, fully fledged as an adult reader, he grew wings and took off with Jorge Luis Borges, with Italo Calvino, with the whole complex fictional riff of stories about stories. It is almost as though his reading has gone full cycle, from the discovery that narrative exists to the dissection of the very concept of story.

And, along the way, a mind matures. Read this book, and you will at once be set thinking about the way in which you too have grown up with books – been built by books. Differently so, of course – we all read differently – but there will be plenty of overlap, plenty of excited recognition. Peter Dickinson – oh yes, *The Blue Hawk*. Joan Aiken – yes, yes. *The Sword in the Stone* – oh, indeed yes. This is what makes cultural community. You think that you are alone with a book; in fact, you become one of a crowd. Which is fine – and each of us will take something different from that book. And grow up differently.

PENELOPE LIVELY once had the temerity to write for children, but has not done so for decades. The Folio Society is about to produce an edition of *The Ghost of Thomas Kempe*, which would astonish her alter ego who wrote it so long ago.

The House that Jack Built

GRANT MCINTYRE

Most people would agree that Patrick O'Brian's Aubrey/Maturin novels, set when Britain's Navy had first Napoleon and then the USA to confront, are among the best historical fiction the twentieth century produced. In fact plenty would drop that word 'among', since the books contain so much variety, perceptiveness and subtle comedy, so many wonderful themes and inventions of genius which add to the fun of reading them. There's the constantly evolving contrast between Jack Aubrey, audacious and tough-minded commander, and his ship's surgeon Stephen Maturin, secretive natural philosopher and political agent. There's the fascination of the ships themselves, complex, almost living things. Also the continuous interplay, like soap opera, among her crew, fighting men shut up together without space or privacy, hundreds or even thousands of miles from land. Some of those men we get to know pretty well. And there's the drama of warfare at sea – or in some weathers just survival at sea – drama so intense the reader nearly forgets to breathe.

Patrick O'Brian's Aubrey/Maturin novels comprise: *Master and Commander* (1969); *Post Captain* (1972); *HMS Surprise* (1973); *The Mauritius Command* (1977); *Desolation Island* (1978); *The Fortune of War* (1979); *The Surgeon's Mate* (1980); *The Ionian Mission* (1981); *Treason's Harbour* (1983); *The Far Side of the World* (1984); *The Reverse of the Medal* (1986); *The Letter of Marque* (1988); *The Thirteen-Gun Salute* (1989); *The Nutmeg of Consolation* (1991); *Clarissa Oakes* (1992); *The Wine-Dark Sea* (1993); *The Commodore* (1994); *The Yellow Admiral* (1996); *The Hundred Days* (1998); *Blue at the Mizzen* (1999); and *The Final Unfinished Voyage of Jack Aubrey* (2004). All are available as paperbacks from HarperCollins.

I wrote a little about these things in Issue 40. But in fact there is much more in the books than war and ships. There is almost the whole of eighteenth-century experience. Likewise, O'Brian's characters are much more than their rôles. We see them pretty complete. Jack, for instance, straightforward and confident at sea, is endearingly helpless on land, his optimism and goodwill undermined by the crudest swindles and frauds, or just by the intricacies of life. Even his friend Stephen, shrewd enough as political agent and spy, can't always read his own heart.

So, while the first article was about life at sea, this one is about life ashore, and the loves of the two men's lives.

Jack marries Sophie Williams, fending off opposition from her widowed mother, who's 'a deeply stupid, griping, illiberal, avid, tenacious, pinchfist lickpenny, a sordid lickpenny and a shrew'. Sophie is not like her mother. She's tall, with wide-set eyes and a wonderful sweetness of expression, a 'reserved creature, living much in an inward dream whose nature she [does] not communicate to anyone'. At one point in their overlong courtship Jack finds himself giving her a lift between ports in his ship. His bumbling efforts to please show an imperfect sense of married reality. He sets his men to make a cabin for her.

> 'Tell me, who of the officers is the most remarkable for taste?'
>
> 'For taste, sir?' cried Simmons.
>
> 'Yes, yes, artistic taste. You know, a sense of the sublime.'
>
> 'Why, sir, I don't know that any of us is much gifted in that line. I do not remember the sublime ever having been mentioned in the gun-room. But there is Mallet, sir, carpenter's crew, who understands these things. He was a receiver of stolen

property, specialising in pretty sublime pieces, as I understand it – old masters and so on . . .'

Sophie is actually not much attuned to the sublime, and anyway the cabin turns out like a brothel, with a touch of undertaker's parlour. Meanwhile, her idea of Jack is as wide of the mark as his of her; for one thing she decides that he can't really love her unless she understands the political scene, and behaves as is right. 'Of course,' she says, asking advice from Stephen, 'I do know it is the French who are so wicked; but there are all these people who keep coming and going – the Austrians, the Spaniards, the Russians. Pray, are the Russians a good thing now? It would be very shocking – treason no doubt – to put the wrong people in my prayers.'

Finally married, Jack and Sophie acquire a damp cottage on wretched land and Jack sets about adding on grand wings and stables – by that means enriching any dishonest tradesmen, charlatans, horse-copers or others who can spot an opportunity. 'Running-horses, cards, building, and even God forbid silver mining,' says Stephen in despair. 'All that lacks is a navigation-canal at ten thousand pound a mile, and the perpetual motion.'

O'Brian gives us a wonderfully subtle sense of a couple who love and respect each other very dearly but never quite become one flesh. Jack feels he has the wrong notion of marriage altogether. 'I had thought there was more friendship and confidence and unreserve in it than the case allows . . . When you are in command, you get so sick of the loneliness, of playing the great man and so on, that you long to break out of it; but in the nature of things it don't seem possible.' Yet probably theirs is as good a marriage as constant absence can support, and it produces a son plus twin girls Jack can't quite tell apart – lively, ignorant children with a one-legged sailor as governess. The passionate Jack does regret Sophie's almost absent-minded lack of interest in sex, and her possessiveness, but at the deepest level each is crucial to the other's life.

Stephen's marriage is far stranger than Jack's, and takes far longer to happen. Diana Villiers is Sophie's cousin, widowed and reluctantly living in the same household. Where Sophie is willowy and languorous, Diana has a 'quick, flashing rhythm . . . for her, style and grace take the place of virtue'. She's spirited and brave, a fine rider and prodigious driver, who would 'send a team of camels through the eye of a needle at a brisk round trot'.

Diana is attractive to any man, even to Jack when the siege of Sophie is making no progress, and she's not one to let morals keep her from living high. Stephen is drawn to her strongly, though he knows he's not attractive in the least, 'has no advantages of person, nor family, nor purse'. It's true she has a trusting fondness for him – though not of the kind he'd prefer, and that is a continuing torture when he's sure his unpossessive love and concern would bring happiness to both. 'She might love careless extravagance, but she would do little or nothing to come by the means of it: certainly nothing against her inclination . . . She hated being pinched and confined; but she hated being commanded even more.'

However, feelings fade in the end if not cherished, and sometime later when Stephen is bringing her back from America, ill and wretched, he sees her in a different light.

> He tried to put a name to his feeling for her but found no word or combination of words. It was certainly not the passion of his earlier days . . . nor did it resemble friendship – his friendship for Jack Aubrey for instance. Affection entered into it, tenderness, and even a kind of complicity, perhaps, as if they had long been engaged in the same pursuit. Possibly the same absurd pursuit of happiness.

Even while thinking such thoughts he has in mind that she's

become an American citizen and that because war has broken out she is now an enemy alien. If he marries her he'll save her from arrest.

> 'Surely [she says] you must know, surely you must feel that any woman, even a woman as battered as I am, must look for something more – more, what shall I say? – more romantic in an offer of marriage? Even if I were to marry you, which is totally inconceivable, I should never, never do so after such a grovelling, such an utterly mundane and businesslike proposal. It is really a question of common good manners, of ordinary civility. Really, Maturin, I wonder at you.'

This, in a manner of speaking, is a yes.

Their marriage is like Jack's and Sophie's, not one of quite perfect happiness. Stephen, always squalid, cannot be house-trained. Diana still adores high living. He decides that if they are to be happy together they must live apart, 'all the more so since Diana was as intransigent as himself and far more apt to fly into a passion about such things as a pancreas in the drawer of the bedside table or orange marmalade ground into the Aubusson'.

Jack muses on the baby that fairly soon follows:

> Why Stephen should be so pleased with a baby I cannot tell. He was born to be a bachelor . . . quite unsuited for marriage, above all for marriage with Diana, a dashing brilliant creature to be sure, a fine horsewoman and a capital hand at billiards and whist, but given to high play and something of a rake – quite often shows her wine – in any case quite improper for Stephen – has nothing to say to books – much more concerned with breeding horses. Yet between them they have produced this baby; and a baby girl at that.

The baby girl though has a disability, perhaps like autism, which prevents her from speaking or responding to others, and though O'Brian's ideas about such things aren't quite in tune with today's, it's clear to anyone who's ever read fiction that Stephen's relationship with Diana won't end in slippers by the fire.

Sophie may be Jack's love, but the Navy is his life. Coping with natural disasters, navigating to small islands in far distant seas, calculating in his head the play of shifting winds and tides, leading his men by force of character – those are second nature to him. But on land, there's almost nothing that he can get right. Apart from shysters to whom for some reason he's given power of attorney, and leaving aside obviously dicey card rings, his main problem is his father. General Aubrey has retired from the Army and is MP for a rotten borough, voting for any measure that may embarrass the government in the hope he'll be bought off with a sinecure. Jack is inevitably tarred with his father's brush and his career suffers badly, since promotion at that time followed from influence and favouritism. But he repays unpaternal treatment with intended kindness, passing on word of stocks he's been tipped off to buy. Any reader can see at once that the word is a trap, and sure enough both father and son are convicted of rigging the market, defrauding the Stock Exchange; it's nakedly political but Jack finds himself sentenced to the pillory and, worse, dismissed the Service. Of course shipmates turn out in force and make the pillory a kind of apotheosis, but even that is no help.

> Stephen saw . . . that the underlying pain was quite untouched . . . The fact of no longer belonging to the Navy counted more than a thousand pillories, the loss of fortune, loss of rank, and loss of future. It was in a way a loss of being, and to those who knew him well it gave his eyes, his whole face, the strangest look.

Not only is Jack out of the Service but his favourite ship, the old but quick and beautiful frigate *Surprise*, objective correlative of his beliefs and aspirations, is to be sold out of the Service too.

Stephen, so intelligent, undemonstrative and coolly unsentimental, is the friend he needs in a predicament like this. Over time he's moved far from his uppers and now can seize a chance to acquire the *Surprise* privately, and through his contacts to have Jack made her captain. She is to be a Letter of Marque, not part of the Navy but operating unofficially and deniably as a privateer, and serving the King's interest in unconventional ways, maybe in collaboration with unacknowledged allies. Her mission is to the other side of the world, and will keep Jack afloat till justice can be done, and naval being officially restored.

A final article on the Aubrey/Maturin novels will follow in Issue 44.

GRANT MCINTYRE, once a publisher and now a sculptor, knows nothing whatever about ships or the sea – except for what he's learned by reading.

Et in Arcadia

JONATHAN SALE

My father was an intellectually austere Cambridge academic, so we never had a copy of *The Wind in the Willows* in the house. No talking toads on *this* family syllabus, thank you! But Kenneth Grahame did feature on our bookshelves in the shape of two late Victorian bestsellers which would otherwise have escaped my notice, as they have done most readers' of late: *The Golden Age* (1895) and *Dream Days* (1898). Neither was turned into a play by A. A. Milne or Alan Bennett, or filmed by Terry Jones. Yet without them there would have been no Toad Hall, no 'poop-pooping' motor cars, no escapes from prison and no epic battle with the stoats and weasels.

These earlier books made Grahame's name. Among their countless readers was Kaiser Wilhelm II, who kept, apart for the Bible, only one book on his yacht: *Dream Days.* Kenneth Grahame was a high-flier at the Bank of England when he wrote these two collections of short stories. They tell of five orphaned brothers and sisters in a rural household who are engaged in a low-level guerrilla war against the uncles and aunts attempting to keep them in order.

Grahame's preface to *The Golden Age* concludes with the Latin tag '*et in Arcadia ego*' and his two volumes were written during what could be called 'Arcadia II', as an unburdened bachelor messing about in boats and fields during long weekends. These realistic accounts of childhood's ups and downs are bathed in the nostalgic

---

Kenneth Grahame, *The Golden Age* (1895) · Aegypan · Pb · 108pp · £6.45 · ISBN 9781603120616; and *Dream Days* (1898) · Hesperus · Pb · 136pp · £8.99 · ISBN 9781843911951.

glow of his own early years. It was the success of these stories that led directly to *The Wind in the Willows.* A female fan made overtures to the popular author and they entered into an unsuitable marriage; the Toad tales began as bedtime stories for their son, which Grahame was encouraged to turn into a book.

The Wind in the Willows is a novel for children which adults enjoy; *The Golden Age* and *Dream Days* are stories for adults which might appeal to children. Certainly they did to this child – I cannot remember them not being part of the furniture, although some of the wit and most of the classical references would at first have escaped me. In these twenty-five delicate sketches, the children sometimes go on epic sea journeys or fight bloody battles – but only in their fertile imaginations. Other stories hinge on small, childish mishaps and misunderstandings.

In 'The Magic of the Ring' the unnamed narrator and his brother lose their promised trip to the circus – only to get their glorious treat after all from a more sympathetic adult. In 'What They Talked About' the dénouement is that the boys never do discover the topics of girls' gossip. '*Dies Irae*' – yes, even some of the titles are in Latin – depicts a household enveloped by a cloud of sadness, caused by a servant learning of the death of her brother and a little girl not receiving a thank-you letter from *her* brother. It is a poignant picture which stays safely this side of sentimentality.

My own favourite comes from *Dream Days.* In '*Mutabile Semper*' the young narrator has an encounter one morning with an intriguing little girl who does indeed turn out to be 'always changeable'. She wheedles out of him the admission that during tedious moments he escapes into a dream landscape featuring a palace full of chocolates and a park with a row of cannons to be fired at his command.

Revealing his secret turns out to be a bad move, since the *jeune fille fatale* bossily rearranges his fantasy world. She dictates the chocolates he will be allowed to eat and silences the nasty cannons. He smells a rat when she asks if there are other boys in this childish paradise;

ominously, she will not promise to be *his* special friend.

He returns in search of her after lunch, only to be wordlessly dismissed. He has been supplanted by a real-life rival, 'a common little beast' of a vicar's son who is fascinating her with one of his ferrets. The narrator slinks off home. *En route*, he escapes to his dream landscape and has his revenge by eating all the chocolate he likes and triumphantly parading all his soldiers and firing off all the guns.

'The Secret Drawer', in *The Golden Age*, is even more delicate. One of the uncles mentions casually that the old bureau in an unused room contains a hidden compartment. This means only one thing to our young hero: 'Bullion, ingots or Spanish dollars'. Again his imagination gallops off. He decides he will pay off a massive debt of four pennies and in other ways share the fortune surely lurking in the antique writing-desk. But the secret drawer which he discovers is, though not empty, disappointingly lacking in ingots. 'My confident little castles were tumbling down like so many card-houses.' However, he takes some cheer from the fact that the contents of the drawer must have been placed there long ago by 'a kindred spirit to my own':

Anna Trench

> a portrait of a monarch unknown to me, cut from some antique print and deftly coloured by hand in just my own bold style of brushwork, some foreign copper coins and a list of birds'-eggs . . . It was a real boy's hoard, then, that I had stumbled upon . . . Across the void stretch of years I seemed to touch hands a moment with my little comrade of seasons – how many seasons? – long since dead.

He carefully replaces the much-loved objects so that some young, kindred spirit in the future will discover them. Then he returns to the present and heads off for the loud game of bears which his siblings are playing down the corridor.

Like his fictional creations, Kenneth Grahame had a parent-free childhood. His mother died when he was very young and his father disappeared into France, drink and death, leaving his children to the care of their forbidding grandmother. Young Kenneth too was free to roam around the countryside. In his stories adults have walk-on, amble-off roles. 'The Olympians', as he terms these remote creatures in his preface to *The Golden Age*, are often incomprehensible and uncomprehending but not deliberately unkind. The servants – these brothers and sisters may have been orphans but they were privileged orphans – are on the side of the children.

Also on-side is the odd (in both senses) adult ready to join in their games, tell stories about talking dragons and let them thump at the piano without bothering with the tedious business of musical notation. These adults sometimes hand out extra pocket-money: 'one – two – three – four half-crowns! . . . I hope he dies tonight, for then he'll go straight to heaven!'

Regretting in his preface that he now has no wish to indulge his childish fantasies, such as letting off explosives on the lawn, Grahame wonders sadly if he too has become an Olympian. The answer at that point seems to have been 'not quite' and his books reflect the landscape and time where part of his mind still dwelt.

For me too they bring back sensations from my own childhood. I experience nostalgia for his nostalgia. A reader coming fresh to these two books will, I hope, find them as intriguing as those cherished objects preserved in the secret drawer by a long-gone kindred spirit. Having introduced them to my own children, I can't wait to pass on the stories to the following generation. However, my grandchildren are still very young, so we'll do some walloping with Toad first.

JONATHAN SALE was the Features Editor of *Punch* until both he and the magazine were axed. He has just edited a new version of a scary Victorian volume on premature burial.

Before Mrs Miniver

VALERIE GROVE

> Many is the letter I might have written if I had not first made a list of the letters I intended to write.

> Giving a party is very like having a baby: its conception is more fun than its completion, and once you have begun it is almost impossible to stop.

With such thoughts Jan Struther first found fame, in the polished little essays she wrote for the *Spectator*, the *New Statesman* and *Punch* in the 1920s and '30s. It was not until 1937 that she created her imaginary middle-class housewife Mrs Miniver for *The Times*, having been invited to brighten up its Court page by Peter Fleming, brother of Ian. He asked her to write about 'an ordinary woman doing ordinary things, a woman like yourself', knowing perfectly well that she was far from ordinary. And when her Mrs Miniver pieces were turned into a fanciful film that won five Oscars, Jan Struther's journalistic career was effectively drowned in Blitz-spirit sentiment.

We may still come across that wartime film, starring the elegant Greer Garson, on a Sunday afternoon. But readers of Slightly Foxed Edition No. 21, *The Real Mrs Miniver*, by Jan Struther's granddaughter Ysenda Maxtone Graham, know that Garson's elegant character was nothing like the mischievously witty author, who preferred wearing dungarees to a cocktail frock.

Try Anything Twice is a collection of her earlier work, first published in 1938. When Virago reprinted it in 1990 I was captivated.

Jan Struther, *Try Anything Twice* (1938), is out of print.

The journalistic essay is an almost period form now (only Katharine Whitehorn still practises it) but Jan Struther's *aperçus* retain their point and sparkle across the century. In the title essay, she characteristically turns on its head the old axiom 'try anything once', suggesting that some things take years to try – 'such as marital fidelity and keeping a diary' – while others, such as infidelity and leaving off keeping the diary, 'are the work of a moment'.

Along with her wit and wisdom, I like her enthusiasms – her longing for solitude in a crowded room, or for her children when they are out of sight; her zest for life ('an accidental gift . . . impossible to acquire, and almost impossible, thank heaven, to lose') and her love of words. She trapped words like butterflies: *sesquipedalian*, *callipygian*, *macrocephalous* – words that 'make the dullest heart dance'. Being able always to find *le mot juste*, she is an effortless read.

I like, too, the fact that she wrote from a domestic perspective, with small children about. Very few women writers before 1960 were acquainted with day-to-day family life, which colours everything (even if, like all women of her class, Jan hired cooks and nannies from Mrs Cattermole's Domestic Agency).

Jan's nom de plume came from her birth-name, Joyce Anstruther – 'J. Anstruther' – though by marriage she was Mrs Anthony Maxtone Graham. In Mrs Miniver she had presented her alter ego as a contented mother of three, living in a Chelsea square (as she herself did, in Wellington Square), observing people's foibles and recording small family crises, just before the Second World War. The keynote of the column was marital compatibility, but this picture was already a sham. In 1940 Jan took her two younger children to America, already in the grip of Miniver-mania and ready to adore her. She delivered three or four lectures per week in 47 states, appeared on radio panel-games, and wrote a patriotic ballad which Eleanor Roosevelt made her husband read on his next broadcast to the nation. In 1943, at the pinnacle of her fame, she stayed with the Roosevelts at the White House. She slept in Abraham Lincoln's bed and pronounced the current president 'a perfectly gorgeous man'.

Meanwhile her husband Tony Maxtone Graham, serving with the Scots Guards, was a prisoner-of-war in Italy; when he came home the marriage was doomed. Jan had fallen in love with a tall, erudite Viennese refugee named Dolf Placzek whom she had met in London in 1938; he was thirteen years younger than her and a foot taller, but they embarked on a passionate affair. They married in 1948 and were happy together for the short time left to Jan, who died of breast cancer in 1952.

The essays in *Try Anything Twice* belong to her charmed 1930s life, and I think my favourite is '– Of A Party'. 'How perfect it is,' she writes, 'that first moment, when one of you says, "It's about time we gave another party," and suddenly the room is full of people, talking, laughing, drinking, the women all beautiful and the men witty. So rosy is the picture that you lose no time in setting the reality in train.' Buying a complete sheet of stamps, in order to send out the invitations, is, she maintains, 'one of the cheapest ways . . . of attaining the sensation of true lordliness'. And awaiting replies is the most agreeable time of all. 'The lover, the party-giver and the free-lance journalist are the only people who feel a genuine interest in the postman's knock.'

In a crescendo of agitation, she describes the day of the party, including the delivery of 250 obscenely large sausage rolls 'designed for the jaws and maws of giants' instead of the 100 delicate, Lilliputian sausage rolls ordered, and the hostess flopping exhausted on her bed just before the first ring of the door-bell, when her heart 'swoops sickeningly downward'. 'And suddenly the party breaks over you like a wave. You throw up your hands and drown.' A faultless summary of the hostess's lot.

In 'Snillocs' she praises the instant friendships that spring up between fellow guests at a country-house weekend, when they slope off together to gossip about the hosts – 'than which there is no more satisfying conversation in the world'. Perhaps for this reason, the ideal house-party is one where the hosts are suddenly called away. And surely, she reasons, it is the hosts who should write thank-you letters to their guests, who have so sportingly undergone this upheaval, this ordeal of packing and travelling, in order to be there? The obligatory thank-yous from guests, named after the oleaginous Mr Collins in *Pride and Prejudice*, could be called 'Snillocs'.

London, for Jan Struther, is like a subtle and expensive scent: it contains repellent ingredients ('fogs, slums, dirt, pneumatic drills'), yet London-dwellers remain helplessly addicted. In 'Paradise Lost', she invokes a Mediterranean holiday, where life is blissful and brandy cheap. Here you may spy a farmhouse to let, also cheap – so why do you not take possession of it? 'I found myself wondering why we had done nothing about that farm; asked no questions, made no effort at all; why one never does do anything; why one always goes back in the end to fogs and offices and wet Saturday nights in the King's Road.'

Her most famous poem begins with the ironical line, 'Now heaven be thanked, I am out of love again!' All her life she wrote crisp, metropolitan lyrics full of memorable observations on love and loss, youth and age. Another, entitled 'At a Dull Party', begins 'In fifty years at most I shall be dead' and ends, 'Then, Christ! what spendthrift folly brought me here – To breathe stale smoke, and drink, talk, think small beer?'

But outlasting her poems and her 'perishable prose' are her hymns. Jan was neither a churchgoer nor a believer, but her friend Canon Percy Dearmer asked her to produce something for his 1925 hymnal, *Songs of Praise*. Being with Canon Dearmer always lifted her spirits, and she found his faith infectious. So she contributed a dozen hymns, all quite inspired. 'When a Knight Won His Spurs' remains a children's favourite; 'Lord of All Hopefulness, Lord of All Joy' is sung movingly at weddings and memorial services; and one of her hymns rather sweetly thanks the Lord 'for dogs with friendly faces'.

Some may feel that her writing, being of its time, has a hint of entitlement to well-heeled privilege. But beneath the prose stylist's phrases, Jan's instincts were socialist. Unlike her husband's Scottish family, she was quite unstuffy, less interested in forebears than in what she called her afterbears. She peppered her talk with four-letter words, which shocked those who expected her to be Miniverish.

'There are few things more embarrassing than to hear people, often in front of the servants . . . dignify their hard-upness with the name of poverty,' she writes; she was well aware of the slums behind her house. The children of 'Pump Lane' subsist on white bread and jam, yet are 'ravishingly beautiful and unreasonably healthy'. (Compare the distaste Mrs Miniver expressed for Really Nice Children in Kensington Gardens, pushed in their sleek perambulators by nannies: 'children who had rocking-horses and special furniture with rabbits on, and grandmothers with houses in the country' – even though her own had all of these.)

I cannot pretend that Jan Struther was ever the chirpy type, looking on the bright side. She fell prey to profound depressions. She was familiar with the zeal for doing household chores that comes with writer's block. But her perceptions are timelessly consoling, especially about the onset of middle-age ('only yesterday one was making a mud-pie,' she reflects, 'and now a contemporary has become a Brigadier-General') accompanied by the sudden appeal of gardening. In 'The Real New Year', she makes a convincing argument for moving Hogmanay to springtime. January is a wretched month of unpayable bills. Surely spring is the time for making resolutions. Seeing the first buds fills us with 'irrational joy', and we resolve 'to write a poem, paint a picture, compose a symphony, found a business, plant a tree, build a summer-house, and re-paper the dining-room . . .' Such thoughts that struck her eighty years ago might occur to any of us today.

VALERIE GROVE was once, like Jan, a mother with small children underfoot while writing for newspapers. Now a grandmother, she is reissuing her biography of Laurie Lee for his centenary this summer.

A Blooming Miracle

GORDON BOWKER

I first encountered James Joyce on the banks of the Suez Canal, a bleak and unpromising setting for any meeting. In one direction lay desert, scorching and soulless, in the other the silhouettes of ships heading majestically like silent ghosts towards ports and harbours unknown. After some years of travel I was returning to England and the prospect of a life among books and sleepy dons, far removed from dismal and dangerous places.

I had acquired the newly published *Penguin Book of Contemporary Verse*, a shrewdly chosen collection which gathered together most of the poets who can still set my pulses racing – Lawrence, Owen, Sassoon, Eliot, Yeats, Auden, Spender, Dylan Thomas and Louis MacNeice, whose poignant 'Prayer before Birth' and deliciously preposterous 'Bagpipe Music' were undoubted *coups de foudre*. But the most incomprehensible piece of nonsense in the anthology was a poem called 'The Ballad of Persse O'Reilly' by 'James Augustine Joyce'. The short profile introducing the poem was the first I ever knew of the life of this strange Irish genius.

So my discovery of Dublin's Dante was not by the usual route, via *A Portrait of the Artist as a Young Man* or *Dubliners* (they came shortly afterwards), but by way of this extract from the bizarre and labyrinthine *Finnegans Wake*, the interior monologue of the slumbering Humphrey Chimpden Earwicker of whom the mysterious Mr O'Reilly is one of several incarnations.

James Joyce, *Ulysses* (1922)
Everyman · Hb · 1,076pp · £14 · ISBN 9781857151008

Back in England, waiting to start university, I was browsing in a provincial bookshop when my eye fell on '*Ulysses* by James Joyce', which I had wrongly imagined to be banned. It was a reprint of the beautifully designed 1936 Bodley Head de luxe edition, with an olive-green cover and Eric Gill's iconic Ulyssean bow running along the spine. And despite its reputation as an 'indecent' book it was unbowdlerized. I now know that Joyce refused to see it published otherwise. It cost a healthy slice of my student grant but was, I thought, a necessary extravagance for any real student of literature.

I still have that copy with its marginal pencillings and endpaper notes, indicating that I must have read it more than once over the years before acquiring a paperback edition, now well-thumbed. One strange thing that quickly caught my eye was that page 7 was nothing but a list of forty-odd errata with corrections. Modern scholars claim to have found very many more. This is perhaps not surprising. Joyce was a compulsive neologist, his pages teeming with verbal conjurations, word puzzles and odd spellings which must have been a nightmare for the printers. In *Finnegans Wake* (see *SF* No. 22), an even more elaborate confection of strange coinages, Joyce and his friend Paul Léon found over 600 which the poor Faber typesetters had misread. (That was in 1940. By 2011, scholars claimed to have detected thousands of misprints.)

But there are other aspects of *Ulysses* which can baffle the unwary reader. Joyce did not rewrite the story of the Greek hero and his adventurous return from Troy to Ithaca. This is the story of a day in the life of the distinctly unheroic Leopold Bloom, an Irish Jew, his cuckolding wife Molly, and Stephen Dedalus, a student in search of an artistic dream and a father-substitute. If there is a tenuous connection to the Greek myth in its eighteen chapters it is not immediately evident.

But, on reading, some parallels do begin to emerge. Bloom is the Ulysses figure; his wife Molly is the book's Penelope, and Stephen its Telemachus. Of course, Bloom's perambulations are not, like

Ulysses', across perilous oceans but around the comparatively peaceful streets of Dublin during one day, 16 June 1904, now celebrated as 'Bloomsday'. But in some fashion the plot does echo the homeward voyage of the Greek hero, with the mythical Sirens, Cyclops, Calypso, Circe and other perils and temptations represented by their equally threatening, alluring and seductive prosaic counterparts.

The book opens with a comically satirical episode set on the roof of the Martello tower at Sandycove just outside Dublin. The main players are Stephen and Buck Mulligan, an irreverent poet, modelled on Joyce's impious and manipulative friend Oliver St John Gogarty. Mulligan mocks Dedalus for having renounced his Catholic faith and refused to kneel at the bedside of his dying mother, despite her pleas. Also in the tower is an Anglo-Irishman called Haynes who has noisy nightmares and, ominously, carries a revolver, and who represents the fanatical nationalism from which Joyce wished to escape.

The progress of our heroes takes us from the Martello tower to a school classroom, a seaside strand, Bloom's kitchen, a funeral, a busy newspaper office, a restaurant, a couple of pubs, a brothel, a cabman's shelter and, finally, to the Blooms' bedroom where Molly is allowed to voice her sometimes lascivious dreamtime thoughts, a chapter usually referred to as the 'Penelope' episode. Joyce had caught and frozen the life and consciousness of the capital of British Ireland on a single day at the turn of the twentieth century, complete with British bobbies, soldiers, red pillar-boxes and a resident Viceroy. 'I want', he said, 'to give a picture of Dublin so complete that if the city suddenly disappeared from the earth it could be reconstructed out of my book.'

It is evident from the outset that there is more to *Ulysses* than meets the eye. For those who enjoy literary puzzles it is a cornucopia rich with allusions – to Catholic liturgy, the Bible, Shakespeare and a whole library of other works. One chapter includes a lively debate about *Hamlet*'s relation to the biographical Shakespeare; in another there's a surreal drama of sado-masochistic fantasies in a Dublin brothel which prefigures the modern Theatre of the Absurd; and in yet another a discussion about procreation conducted in a fireworks display of English literary styles from Chaucer to the popular press. This stylistic virtuosity, with which Joyce began toying in *A Portrait of the Artist*, often left the dullest critics baffled. A passage attempting to recapture his earliest childhood memories, couched in the style of a sentimental Victorian novel, prompted one of its more simple-minded critics to describe it as 'scrupulously pumped out 19th-century bilge'. But T. S. Eliot saw it for what it was – 'marvellous parody' from a 'subtle, erudite, even massive' mind.

Joyce enjoyed creating obscurity, famously telling a would-be French translator of *Ulysses*, 'I've put in so many enigmas and puzzles that it'll keep the professors busy for centuries arguing over what I meant.' But one is not obliged to probe for deep meanings in this or any other of Joyce's novels in order to enjoy them. He was a fine singer and both his poetry and his prose have a musical quality, as if deliberately written to be sung. So his prose is often better listened to than read.

Ulysses is also a book to dip into like a poetry anthology, just to enjoy the satire, savour the language and delight in the symphony of sound the words produce. It is the approach to his work which many of his most sympathetic early critics recommended and it remains the best advice on how to tackle the novel.

Joyce was probably the first novelist to use in any sustained fashion the stream of consciousness, a prose version of the dramatic soliloquy which enabled him to enter into a character's thoughts or switch from one consciousness to another. Occasionally, for effect, he shifts from first- to third-person narrative or to dramatic dialogue. This can take the reader from the thought-stream of the philosophical Stephen to the more prosaic mind of Bloom preoccupied with his morning ablutions, the dreams of an adolescent girl couched in the language of the cheap romance, and finally to Molly Bloom's famous meditation. It is a merry-go-round: two men's meandering steps around the city and one woman's meandering thoughts around her psyche, with many Dublinesque characters dancing in and out.

The book itself had an unusually adventurous career. Joyce conceived it originally as a short story while working briefly as a bank clerk in Rome in 1906. Over the next sixteen years it was written and rewritten, but it ran into trouble almost as soon as parts of it were published. Episodes were printed serially in two magazines – the *Egoist*, edited in London by Harriet Shaw Weaver, who became Joyce's patron, and the *Little Review*, edited in New York by Jane Heap and Margaret Anderson. Heap and Anderson were prosecuted and fined for publishing one extract considered obscene by the American courts, and Weaver was unable to find a printer willing to risk prosecution by setting it up in type.

Ulysses was finally rescued by another intrepid woman, Sylvia Beach, whose Left Bank English-language bookshop, Shakespeare and Company, was a favourite haunt of British, American and French writers in post-war Paris. Finally, on Joyce's fortieth birthday, 2 February 1922, the first uncensored edition appeared under the Shakespeare and Company colophon.

But in America it was banned until 1934 when even the climate in Britain had begun to change. A small deluxe edition was published in England in 1936 by the dashing young Allen Lane, who somehow managed to outmanoeuvre the Home Office and avoid prosecution, though it did not appear in a trade edition until December 1937. By that time Lane had left Bodley Head to launch Penguin Books, which, 23 years later, almost to the day, published the unexpurgated *Lady Chatterley's Lover*. This time the Home Office pounced and that book became the centre of a celebrated court case.

Ulysses had a mixed reception. Catholic reactions were hostile; the *Sporting Times* declared, 'It is enough to make a Hottentot sick'; Virginia Woolf's first reaction, tempered later, was 'An illiterate, underbred book', the work of 'a queasy undergraduate scratching his pimples'; while W. B. Yeats called it 'the work of an heroic mind'.

For Joyce this was the book of his life in several ways. It incorporated real characters he knew and real events in which he had taken part. It also marked the passage of a superb creative imagination from writing lyrical verse, clever short stories and a revealing autobiographical novel to its penultimate and most sophisticated expression. Furthermore, it celebrated the day on which Joyce first walked out with his wife-to-be, Nora Barnacle, his chief model for Molly Bloom.

Joyce never returned to Ireland after writing *Ulysses*, fearing his reception in so devoutly Catholic a country. But, as he said, and as his friends recognized, that was the focus of his genius, especially Dublin. Returning to an Ireland no longer British but now dominated by narrow-minded nationalists and an unforgiving Church would have meant returning to a different place from the one that had inspired him. Probably no city has been so celebrated in English literature apart from Dickens's London.

But unlike Dickens's London, Joyce's Dublin is still largely recognizable and you can easily retrace the footsteps of the various characters and visit most of the scenes in the novels and stories. Consequently the city attracts many Joyce enthusiasts as well as those puzzled professors, especially on 'Bloomsday'. As with many great writers there's an industry of scholarship focusing on Joyce and shelves of books attempting to explain his fiction or exploring his life and times. But, like those of most great writers, the best books about Joyce are those he wrote himself.

GORDON BOWKER has written biographies of Malcolm Lowry, Lawrence Durrell and George Orwell. A major biography of Joyce appeared in 1952, which some considered the last word on the author. Gordon Bowker was foolhardy enough to challenge that view with his *James Joyce: A Biography* (2011).

The drawing of James Joyce on p. 86 is reprinted by permission of David R. Godine, Publisher, Inc., from Roberto Vicq de Cumptich, *Men of Letters and People of Substance*.

Turning a Page

GLYN FREWER

My father was a bibliophile, a bibliographer and a university librarian for fifty years, and I cannot remember a time when I was without books. It was inevitable, therefore, that I should grow up with an ambition to own and run a bookshop. After thirty years in advertising, I bought a small haberdashery called Stuff & Nonsense in Stow-on-the-Wold. I stripped it of all the racks, previously filled with green anoraks, rolls of furniture fabric, strange hats with ear-flaps that pulled down or bobbles that stood up, shooting-sticks, carved thumb-sticks and pink wellingtons, and fitted it out with bookshelves.

I had already amassed a heterogeneous collection of about a thousand books so that I wouldn't open with empty shelves. I sat at a small desk facing the front door and the window, where I displayed a varied selection of come-hither titles. An Austrian cow-bell jangled bucolically every time the door opened; in the desk drawer, a cigar-box served as a till and a Balkan Sobranie tobacco tin held coins for change. I was ready.

Customers began to trickle in, encouraging me by saying they were pleased that a second-hand bookshop had opened in the town. Many came in (including the then Foreign Secretary) with plastic bags filled with books they had been waiting to get rid of, and before long I was being asked to visit the homes of people who were about to move, to help them clear out their books. Reinforced by a lifetime of browsing in second-hand bookshops, I found I had little difficulty in judging how to price them.

But not all the time. A small booklet published in India, *The Art of Taxidermy: Mounting the Tiger* by G. and M. Patel, I had priced at 50p. A lady (and she really was, she was titled) seized the book from the shelves with a cry of delight.

'How extraordinary! These two brothers stuffed all my husband's trophies. I must take this. How much is it?'

I indicated the pencilled price.

'Is that all? I'd have paid £50 for this. Thank you so much.'

The cow-bell rang out the departure of one very satisfied customer, and now I had a coin to rattle in my box.

But I had also learned an invaluable lesson. If a book on tiger-stuffing could sell like a hot cake in Stow-on-the-Wold, it proved there was a buyer for any and every book; it was just a matter of bringing the two together. From then on I bought arcane and esoteric titles I would previously have ignored, and never regretted it.

Within a few weeks, I quickly learned which categories of books and which authors I should concentrate on. I reduced the size of the fiction section; the ubiquitous charity shops provided greater choice. I enlarged the sections of my own special interests – the countryside and children's books – which remained the largest in the shop, and I also increased religion, cookery, handicrafts, history (especially military history) and biography. Literature was a large section from the start. I learned that demand for the works of Scott, Thackeray, Galsworthy and Hope was negligible but that there was a ready market for Jane Austen, the Brontës, Dickens, Hardy, Trollope, Tolstoy, Waugh and Graham Greene. Poetry was always in demand. I kept two shelves of mixed uncategorized books so that customers could make their own discoveries. I filled boxes with ephemera: postcards, bookmarks (a silk-woven one by Stevens of Birmingham fetched £25), cigarette cards, prints, even a set of glass lantern slides.

As the weeks, months and years went by, enjoyment grew. My initial plan of bridging for a couple of years that life-changing transition between being employed and answerable to others and being retired and beholden to no one went by the board. I enlarged the shop,

B. Lodge

converting the first floor, partitioning off the sink to form a mini-kitchen and adding shelves for a few more thousand books. Then I converted the attic space for another few thousand. My stock capacity increased from the original 3,000 to 10,000 with the result that I stayed happily trading for sixteen years.

Every day was different. American tourists flocked to Stow and became valued customers. All were delightful to talk to, especially the better-read of whom there were many. A few let the side down. After a lengthy browse through the literature shelves, one approached the desk with a book in his hand, Samuel Johnson's *Lives of the English Poets*. 'Say, this guy didn't cover the best ones, did he? There's no Keats, no Shelley, no Wordsworth.'

In my second year I had a telephone call which resulted in one of my most successful buying coups. A newly arrived librarian at a long-established boarding-school wanted to clear out all the Victorian leather-bound tomes from the school library to make room for new books. I was invited to make an offer for any book I wanted. The outcome was several car-loads of leather-bound sets of *The Edinburgh Review*, *Household Words*, *The Quiver*, *Punch*, *The Encyclopaedia Britannica* and *The Quarterly Review*, as well as works by Ward Fowler, Richard Jefferies and W. H. Hudson. Within a couple of months, I had sold them all. The leather-bound ones were the first to go, some to local antique shops to decorate their windows, many to Americans who seemed to love any book bound in leather.

The Stow horse fair, which is held each May and October, was a mixed blessing. The influx of a thousand or so gypsies and New Age travellers caused many shops to close, though I stayed open. I always kept back a batch of paperback Westerns for one gypsy family who liked to read them in the winter, and during one fair I had a memorable visit. Two customers, in their early twenties, long-haired, clad in black and smelling pungently of wood-smoke, entered the shop. I was on edge, hoping they wouldn't cause trouble, as they browsed along the shelves, one on each side of the shop. The woman turned to address her companion.

'Darling, he's got some George Borrow.'

'Has he, sweetie? Get *Lavengro* if it's there, would you?'

In fact they bought several books, and they taught me a vital lesson: never judge by appearances – or pungency.

There was one aspect of the book trade that I had to learn from scratch: dealing with first editions. Fortunately, I had subscribed to a monthly magazine, *Book & Magazine Collector*, which dealt with individual authors and their works, and current market prices. The magazine was invaluable, preventing me from making serious mistakes. Chatting with collectors themselves taught me a lot, and there was a lot to learn. The discrimination and fastidiousness which collectors exercise in pursuit of their quarry always amazed me. A first edition had to be pristine, without a mark, a scuff, a blemish of any kind, and the same applied to the dust-jacket. I had a fine first edition of Golding's *Lord of the Flies* without a jacket, which I sold for £40. Sometime later, I sold an identical edition with its pristine jacket for £240. The value of that piece of paper was £200 and I soon became wise to the stratagems of some collectors. A later edition of a book would often be published with a jacket identical to that of the first edition. A later edition was cheap. The wrapper was transferred to the jacketless first edition and the value rocketed.

There were two aspects of the book trade that always made me uneasy. First editions of children's books fetched a high price, yet to me it seemed that children's books were meant for children. This would all too often be brought home to me.

'Mum, there's a *Rupert* annual here. It's only £95. Can I have it?'

The other was the dilemma posed by selling books with hand-coloured plates, most commonly found in pre-twentieth-century natural history books, to customers you knew were print-dealers.

They would detach the plates, mount them and sell them individually for anything from £10 to £50 or more. Each volume of Jardine's Natural History Library, for example, contains thirty hand-coloured plates. From one volume, a print-dealer could make £300 at the very least. (The plates in the volumes *Parrots* and *Pigeons*, both by Edward Lear, could bring a return of £1,000 or more.) The market price for a single volume was £40. The print-dealers' argument was that more people would see and enjoy the plates on their walls at home than would ever be likely to see them in old books, but that argument did not ease my conscience.

These aspects apart, what possible reason could I ever have had for giving up this life of bibliophilic bliss? There was no single reason. But I did have an increasing sense of foreboding, which clouded my vision of the future. More and more customers would come in and browse, find a book they wanted and then say they would just check it out on Amazon. I judged the time was right to ease myself out of this wonderfully satisfying and enjoyable occupation.

I sold my business as a going concern and I hope that this kind of shop will continue to have a place in the world, albeit a smaller one than hitherto. For what other way of life is there where, if trade is slow, you can pursue your love of reading, and if trade is busy, you know that anyone who steps over the threshold is a kindred spirit? You talk about books, exchange opinions, compare, reminisce and pass the time of day discussing a mutual love. I enjoyed all this for sixteen years. What more could any book-lover want?

The leaving card GLYN FREWER's advertising agency gave him on retirement bore a cartoon captioned: 'Books Bought, Books Sold, Books Written, Book Mad' – which was about right.

Bibliography

Max Beerbohm, *Zuleika Dobson* 59

Barbara Comyns, *Our Spoons Came from Woolworths*; *The Vet's Daughter*; *A Touch of Mistletoe* 19

Lawrence Durrell, *Prospero's Cell*; *Bitter Lemons of Cyprus* 30

Jim Ede, *A Way of Life: Kettle's Yard* 24

Kenneth Grahame, *The Golden Age*; *Dream Days* 74

Richard Hughes, *A High Wind in Jamaica* 41

James Joyce, *Ulysses* 83

Irma Kurtz, *The Great American Bus Ride* 49

John Moore, *Portrait of Elmbury* 13

Mary Norton, *The Borrowers*; *The Borrowers Afield*; *The Borrowers Afloat*; *The Borrowers Aloft*; *The Borrowers Avenged* 7

Patrick O'Brian, *Master and Commander*; *Post Captain*; *HMS Surprise*; *The Mauritius Command*; *Desolation Island*; *The Fortune of War*; *The Surgeon's Mate*; *The Ionian Mission*; *Treason's Harbour*; *The Far Side of the World*; *The Reverse of the Medal*; *The Letter of Marque*; *The Thirteen-Gun Salute*; *The Nutmeg of Consolation*; *Clarissa Oakes*; *The Wine-Dark Sea*; *The Commodore*; *The Yellow Admiral*; *The Hundred Days*; *Blue at the Mizzen*; *The Final Unfinished Voyage of Jack Aubrey* 67

Francis Spufford, *The Child that Books Built* 62

Jan Struther, *Try Anything Twice* 78

Wei Jingsheng, *The Courage to Stand Alone: Letters from Prison and Other Writings* 35

E. O. Wilson, *Biophilia* 54

Coming attractions . . .

SIMON BARNES meets a family and other animals

MELISSA HARRISON walks with Rackham

WILLIAM PALMER is kidnapped

MICHELE HANSON marries out

ROHAN CANDAPPA wakes up in Slumberland

YSENDA MAXTONE GRAHAM goes back to school

JUSTIN MAROZZI travels to Burma with Norman Lewis